HERALDS *of the* REFORMATION

Thanks to Kathleen Hannula, Laurel McCoy and Michael Pfefferle for their proof-reading and suggestions for improvement.

Published by Canon Press
P.O. Box 8729, Moscow, Idaho 83843
800.488.2034 | www.canonpress.com

Library of Congress Cataloging-in-Publication Data:
Hannula, Richard M., author.
Heralds of the Reformation : thirty biographies of sheer grace /
   Richard M. Hannula.
Moscow : Canon Press, 2019. | Originally published: 2016.
LCCN 2019029492 | ISBN 9781944503468 (paperback)
LCSH: Reformation—Biography—Juvenile literature.
Classification: LCC BR316 .H36 2019 | DDC 270.6092/2 [B]—dc23
LC record available at https://lccn.loc.gov/2019029492
          19 20 21 22 23 24 25 26   9 8 7 6 5 4 3 2 1

HERALDS *of the* REFORMATION

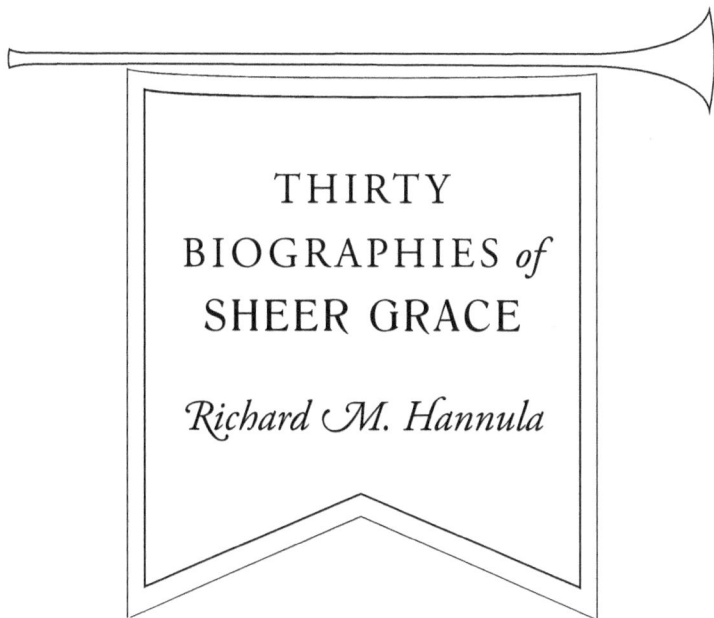

THIRTY BIOGRAPHIES *of* SHEER GRACE

Richard M. Hannula

canonpress
Moscow, Idaho

With love to my grandchildren.

CONTENTS

PART TWO

THE REFORMATION IN GERMANY, SWEDEN, AND THE NETHERLANDS 49

PART THREE

THE REFORMATION IN FRANCE, SWITZERLAND, AND ITALY 115

EPHESIANS 2:8–9

For by grace you have been saved through faith.
And this is not your own doing; it is the gift of God,
not a result of works, so that no one may boast.

HEIDELBERG CATECHISM QUESTION 60

Question: How are you right with God?

Answer: Only by true faith in Jesus Christ. Even though my conscience accuses me of having grievously sinned against all God's commandments and of never having kept any of them, and even though I am still inclined toward all evil, nevertheless, without my deserving it at all, out of sheer grace, God grants and credits to me the perfect satisfaction, righteousness, and holiness of Christ, as if I had never sinned nor been a sinner, as if I had been as perfectly obedient as Christ was obedient for me. All I need to do is to accept this gift of God with a believing heart.

INTRODUCTION

The Protestant Reformation was a great spiritual awakening of faith in Christ that swept across Europe in the 1500s. The Spirit of God stirred the hearts and minds of Martin Luther, Ulrich Zwingli, John Calvin and countless others to rediscover the Christ of the Scriptures and the message that sinners are saved by God's grace when they trust in Christ's sacrifice for their sins.

However, for centuries the good news of Christ had been distorted and overlaid with layers of unbiblical teaching and false practices. The Church of Rome taught that salvation came by believing in Christ and earning merit with God through good works. It declared that Christ's death on the cross did not fully pay the penalty for His people's sin, but that believers must still be purged of their sins after death by a long period of punishment in a place called purgatory to be made fit for heaven. Although the Scriptures clearly teach that "There is one God, and there is one mediator between God and men, the man Christ Jesus" (1 Tim. 2:5), the

1

Roman church taught the people to pray to Mary and the saints in heaven to intercede for them with God. Most medieval parishioners offered more prayers to Mary and the saints than to the Lord God Himself, and they believed the church's teaching that God's blessing came to those who venerated relics, adorned images and made pilgrimages to holy shrines. "As often as I read the Bible," one German bishop said, "I find in it a different religion from that which we are taught."

When the congregation came to church, they watched an elaborate ritual that the priest performed in Latin——a language they did not understand. Most parishioners did not hear sermons that explained to them the truths of the Word of God. In fact, in many regions the Church of Rome barred the common people from reading the Scriptures in their own language. The church instructed the people that salvation and grace came to them through the sacraments, and therefore their spiritual lives depended on the priests who alone could administer the sacraments. God had granted the pope and his ministers the keys to the gates of heaven, the church taught. To challenge their authority was to challenge God.

By the sixteenth century, greed and corruption had choked the spiritual life out of many clergymen. The pope and most bishops lived lives of luxury in regal palaces and showed little concern for the poor. When Leo X became pope in 1513, he declared, "Now that we have attained the papacy, let us enjoy it!" Church offices were sold to the highest bidder. Indulgence salesmen——endorsed by church officials——told anxious crowds that they could relieve the sufferings of their departed loved ones in purgatory by buying indulgences. Money-grubbing and immoral priests and monks set a terrible example for the flock. Bishops imposed heavy ministry taxes on the people, and priests demanded fees for everything.

Through the years, when brave critics pointed out the unbiblical beliefs and practices of the church, church authorities accused them of heresy, and many of the accused suffered imprisonment, torture and even death by burning.

But at a time when the church had drifted farthest from the teachings and practices of the New Testament, a revival of classical learning and the wide-spread use of the printing press prepared the way for reform. The Renaissance and its appreciation for the art and literature of ancient Greece and Rome had begun to transform university education in Europe. Scholars sought knowledge from original sources. Instead of relying on the teachings of medieval theologians to understand the Scriptures, they studied the New Testament in its original Greek and sought out the straightforward meaning of biblical texts. Many——like Thomas Bilney in Cambridge, England——discovered a welcoming Savior, not an aloof judge. "At last I heard Jesus," Bilney said. "Christ alone saves His people from their sins. I came to Christ, and my despairing heart leapt for joy."

In 1517, when Martin Luther nailed his Ninety-five Theses against indulgences on a church door in Wittenberg, Germany, he expected a scholarly discussion among the churchmen of Wittenberg. Instead, printers published his theses and within weeks monks, noblemen and peasants hotly debated the theses throughout Europe. At about the same time that Luther understood the doctrine of justification by faith taught in the Scriptures, reformers in France, Switzerland, England and elsewhere also found the Bible's message of forgiveness in Christ alone. These reformers did not claim to have discovered something new. On the contrary, they made it clear that they simply believed the gospel of Jesus Christ as it is revealed in the Scriptures. The Protestant reformers tried to call the church back to the biblical Christianity of the New Testament church. But officials of the Church of Rome rejected the call and fiercely persecuted the courageous heralds of the Reformation who risked their lives to proclaim the good news of Christ. By God's grace, they led millions of people to a living faith in Jesus Christ and restored the churches of many lands to the Scriptures and to biblical worship.

The following sketches simply scratch the surface of these reformers' lives. Effort was made to honestly depict them in the midst of their unique time and circumstances. However, it was not possible within a few pages to thoroughly explore their teachings and their strengths and weaknesses. To learn much more about these reformers see "For Further Reading" at the end of the book. It is my hope that the reader——boy or girl, man or woman——will be inspired, by the grace of God, to follow in their steps as they followed in Christ's.

OVERVIEW AND TIMELINE

SIXTEENTH CENTURY DIVISIONS OF THE WESTERN CHURCH

Roman Catholics—members of the Church of Rome—recognized the bishop of Rome, the pope, as the supreme head of the church, the leader of a hierarchy of bishops and priests. Although the church accepted the Scriptures as the divinely inspired Word of God, it placed church tradition on an equal footing with the Scriptures. Among the church's central teachings were:

- Sinners achieve salvation through faith in Christ and by earning merit with God through good works.

- Believers must still be purged from their sins after they die by suffering punishment for their sins in a place called purgatory to make them fit for heaven.

- God's grace is bestowed on believers by priests through the seven sacraments.

- The worship service——the mass——is to be conducted in Latin and is a ritual offering of Christ as a sacrifice to God the Father and includes the celebration of the Eucharist where the bread and wine are transformed into the physical body and blood of Christ.

- The faithful should venerate and pray to Mary and the saints, seeking their intercession for God's blessing.

- The church controls the Treasury of Merit, the store of merits earned by the extraordinary good works of Christ and the saints which can be applied to believers through indulgences.

Protestants or Evangelicals accepted the Scriptures alone as the supreme authority for Christian doctrine and life. They rejected the pope as the head of the church and Roman church tradition that was contrary to the Scriptures. In the early decades of the Reformation, the supporters of reform were called "Evangelicals." They earned the nickname because they lived to spread the good news of the gospel—called the *evangelium* in the Latin Bible. In 1529, at an imperial assembly of the Holy Roman Empire, the emperor's government tried to stop the spread of the Reformation by insisting that the Evangelical princes return the churches in their lands to the authority of the Church of Rome. The Evangelical German princes lodged a formal protest against the decree. Afterward, the supporters of the Reformation were often called Protestants. Among the Evangelicals' central teachings were:

- Salvation is entirely God's work by grace alone. God declares believers in Christ forgiven and righteous in His sight based only on the perfect obedience and sacrifice of Jesus Christ in their place——believers cannot contribute to it by their own good works.

- Prayer and adoration are to be given to God alone.

- All believers have direct access to God through Christ. They do not need a priest as a mediator of God's grace.

- The Scriptures should be widely available to the people in their own language.

- Worship services should be conducted in the language of the people and ordered according to the Scriptures.

- Christ instituted only two sacraments: baptism and the Lord's Supper.

The Evangelicals disagreed with one another on the precise meaning of the Lord's Supper and on church government. They also lived in distinct geographic regions under different political leaders and forms of government. Consequently, three main branches of Protestantism developed during the Reformation: Lutheranism in Germany and Scandinavia; Reformed in Switzerland, France, the Netherlands, Scotland and parts of Germany; and Anglicanism in England.

THE MONARCHS
The Holy Roman Empire, Spain and the Netherlands

Charles V (King of Spain, emperor of the Holy Roman Empire, ruler of the Netherlands, 1516–1556), a devout follower of the Church of Rome who brutally suppressed Protestants in Spain, Italy and the Netherlands. He declared Martin Luther an outlaw and demanded that German Protestants return to the Church of Rome. But Charles had his hands full with wars with France and with the Muslim armies of the Ottoman Turks who overran large swathes of eastern and central Europe. Therefore, he made concessions to the German Protestants to win their support against his foreign enemies.

In 1546, when Charles had dealt with the outside threats to his empire, he attacked the German Protestants, invaded their lands and captured their key leaders. A few years later, the defeated Protestant princes made an alliance with King Henry II of France and drove the emperor's forces from their territories. Reluctantly, Charles ratified an agreement that recognized the Protestant faith in those lands.

Frederick the Wise (Elector of Saxony, 1486–1525), a powerful German prince, one of the seven electors who elected the Holy Roman emperor, founded the University of Wittenberg and appointed Martin Luther and Philip Melanchthon as professors. When the pope condemned Luther's teachings and Emperor Charles placed him under the imperial ban, Frederick protected him. After the Diet of Worms in 1521, when Luther refused to recant his teachings before the emperor and high officials of the Church of Rome, Frederick kept Luther from the clutches of the emperor.

John Frederick I (Elector of Saxony, 1532– 1547) embraced the teachings of Martin Luther and promoted the Evangelical faith in his realm. He defended the Augsburg Confession and strongly supported the Schmalkaldic League, a military alliance of the German Protestant states. In 1547, John Frederick was captured by the emperor's forces at the battle of Muhlberg and sent into exile. Although he was offered his freedom if he renounced his Evangelical faith, he refused to do so. In 1552, when the German Protestants successfully rebelled against Charles V, John Frederick was released from captivity.

Philip of Hesse (Landgrave of Hesse, 1518–1567), an Evangelical German prince who, with John Frederick I, rallied the German Protestant states to form an alliance known as the Schmalkaldic League to protect themselves against Emperor Charles V's efforts to eradicate Protestantism from Germany.

When a dispute about the Lord's Supper threatened Protestant unity, Philip held a meeting of the key Evangelical theologians at his castle in Marburg——including Luther, Melanchthon, Bucer and Zwingli——to discuss the issue. Philip encouraged the men to unite as brothers. Unfortunately, his efforts failed. In 1547, when the forces of Charles V defeated the Schmalkaldic League, Philip was captured and held prisoner for five years.

Philip II (King of Spain and Portugal and ruler of the Netherlands, 1556–1598), a strident Roman Catholic who called for the torture and execution of Protestants, effectively wiped out the Evangelical witness in Spain and Portugal. His father, Charles V, arranged his marriage with Mary I of England, but when Mary died childless, Philip lost his right to the English throne, and Mary's half-sister Elizabeth became queen. In 1566, the Protestants of the Netherlands rebelled against his rule which sparked a bloody war for independence that dragged on for decades. When Queen Elizabeth's forces aided the Dutch Protestants and plundered Spanish treasure ships, Philip sent an invasion fleet known as the Spanish Armada to conquer England. A fierce storm and a determined English navy defeated the Armada in 1588, cheering Evangelicals throughout Europe.

France

Francis I (King of France, 1515–1547) was a gifted scholar and a patron of the arts who encouraged the study of Greek and Hebrew. His sister Margaret, Queen of Navarre, supported Lefevre and other

Evangelical scholars, and she urged her brother to reform the church in France. At first, when the French bishops demanded that the king arrest and execute Evangelicals—called Huguenots in France—he refused. But later, when he saw the Huguenots as a threat to the unity of his kingdom, the burning of Huguenots began. Most Evangelical leaders, including Lefevre, Farel and Calvin, fled the country. In order to weaken his chief enemy, Emperor Charles V, Francis made short-lived alliances with the German Protestants and even with the Ottoman Turks. Near the end of his reign, he ordered the annihilation of the Waldensians living in the French Alps.

Henry II (King of France, 1547–1559) followed in the footsteps of his father Francis I and waged war against Charles V. A zealous defender of the Church of Rome, Henry fiercely persecuted the Huguenots, executing hundreds of them and causing thousands to flee France for Switzerland and Germany. He created special courts to deal with the Huguenots, and he called on French citizens to spy on their neighbors and report any Huguenot activities to the police. Despite the persecution, the number of Huguenots grew. They met secretly and were led by pastors trained by John Calvin in Geneva. When Henry died suddenly, he left his wife, Catherine de Medici, with four young heirs to the throne. A massacre of Huguenots by Roman Catholic troops in 1562 led to civil wars that raged for years.

Henry IV (King of France, 1589–1610), the son of a duke descended from a line of French kings and Jeanne d'Albret, the Protestant queen of Navarre, was raised Protestant in the midst of the civil war between Huguenots and Roman Catholics. He fought with the Protestant armies until a peace treaty was signed in 1570 that promised the Huguenots freedom of worship. To strengthen the peace, a marriage was arranged between Henry and a Roman Catholic princess of the

French royal house. On the day of their wedding in Paris in August 1572, King Charles IX ordered the slaughter of thousands of French Protestants—the St. Bartholomew's Day Massacre.

The massacre renewed the civil war. When the French king died in 1589 without an heir, Henry became king of France. But many Roman Catholic noblemen refused to accept a Protestant king, and war raged on for nine more years. In order to end the bloodshed, secure his crown and reunify the war-ravaged kingdom, Henry converted to Roman Catholicism. In 1598, he issued the Edict of Nantes, which retained the Church of Rome as the state church but granted religious freedom to Huguenots.

England

Henry VIII (King of England, 1509–1547) in the early days of the Reformation wrote a book against Luther. When Henry's brother died, Henry married his widow, Catherine of Aragon. Catherine had many miscarriages and one daughter that survived. Henry, anxious to have a male heir, believed that God had cursed their offspring because he had married his brother's wife. Henry tried to get the pope to annul his marriage, but the pope refused. Eventually, Henry broke with the Church of Rome and divorced Catherine. Parliament declared the king "Supreme Head of the Church of England." Henry dissolved the monasteries in the kingdom and confiscated their land and treasure. Despite his split from the pope, Henry did not want to break with the doctrines and practices of the Roman church. Reformers had to patiently win concessions from him to permit the Scriptures to be published in English and to adopt Protestant doctrines like justification by faith in Christ alone.

Edward VI (King of England, 1547–1553) was crowned at the age of nine. His father, Henry VIII, had arranged for Protestant nobles to run the government as regents until Edward came of age. Edward, a bright and diligent student of the Scriptures, embraced the Evangelical faith. His regents and Archbishop Cranmer, with Edward's blessing, reformed the Church of England in ways his father was unwilling to do. The *Book of Common Prayer* replaced the Latin mass, giving the people for the first time a worship service entirely in English. Images of Mary and the saints were removed from the churches and wooden tables replaced stone altars for the celebration of the Lord's Supper. Ministers were allowed to get married. The young king died at the age of fifteen.

Mary I (Queen of England, 1553–1558) ascended the throne after the death of her Protestant half-brother Edward VI. A determined Roman Catholic and the only child of Henry VIII and his first wife, Mary took steps to return England to the Church of Rome. She instigated a fierce persecution of Protestants, and thousands fled the country. Three hundred Protestants were burned at the stake, including many prominent Evangelical leaders—among them Thomas Cranmer, Hugh Latimer and John Bradford. These executions earned her the nickname "Bloody Mary." Her persecution of Protestants and her marriage to Philip II of Spain turned the English people against her. She died in the fifth year of her reign.

Elizabeth I (Queen of England, 1558–1603) became queen when her half-sister Mary died. Elizabeth restored the Protestant faith in the kingdom, but she insisted in following a middle way between Roman Catholic rituals and the worship practices supported by the bolder Protestant reformers. The Act of Supremacy of 1559 declared Elizabeth "Supreme Governor of the Church of England," and the Act of Uniformity forced all citizens to follow the worship ceremonies laid down by church officials in a revised *Book of Common Prayer*.

Ministers and parishioners who pressed Elizabeth and her church leaders to purify the church of unbiblical practices became known as Puritans. Elizabeth fiercely resisted the Puritans' reform efforts and ejected hundreds of Puritan ministers from their churches.

Scotland

Mary, Queen of Scots (Queen of Scotland, 1542–1567) was the daughter of King James V and Mary of Guise, a French princess. When her father died a week after she was born, the infant Mary was proclaimed queen and her mother served as regent on her behalf. In 1558, she married King Francis II of France. When he died a year later, Mary returned to Scotland as a nineteen-year-old widow. By this time, Scotland had become a Protestant country, and Mary, a Roman Catholic, disliked the independent nature of the Church of Scotland. She married a Scottish nobleman who was murdered shortly after the birth of their son James, and Mary was suspected as having been involved in his death. Protestant nobles forced Mary to abdicate in favor of her infant son. She fled to England, but when a plot by Roman Catholic noblemen to assassinate Queen Elizabeth and install Mary as queen of England was discovered, Mary was executed.

James VI (King of Scotland, 1567–1625 and King of England, 1603–1625), the son of Mary, Queen of Scots, was raised Protestant. Evangelical nobles ran the government as his regents until he came of age. As James grew older, he came to believe that he ruled by divine right. Through the years, he tried to assert his authority over the Church of Scotland and frequently clashed with church leaders. When Queen Elizabeth of England died childless, James was the nearest heir to the throne. In 1603, he was crowned King James I of England, thus unifying the crowns of England and Scotland.

REFORMATION TIMELINE

1516 Erasmus published the Greek New Testament

1517 Martin Luther posted the *Ninety-five Theses*

1519 Ulrich Zwingli began preaching in Zurich

1521 Diet of Worms; Luther was excommunicated and declared an outlaw in the empire

1522 Martin Luther published the New Testament in German

1523 Jacques Lefevre published the New Testament in French; Johann Esch and Hendrich Voes became the first martyrs of the Protestant Reformation

1526 William Tyndale published the New Testament in English; Olaf Petri published the New Testament in Swedish

1528 Patrick Hamilton martyred in Scotland

1529 Marburg Colloquy

1530 *Augsburg Confession* signed by German princes

1531 Swedish King Gustavus declared Sweden Protestant; Ulrich Zwingli died; Thomas Bilney martyred

1534 Act of Supremacy declared Henry VIII supreme head of the Church of England

1533 Thomas Cranmer consecrated as the first Protestant archbishop of Canterbury

1536 Dissolution of the monasteries began in England; John Calvin published the *Institutes of the Christian Religion*; Geneva became Protestant; Calvin began his ministry in Geneva; William Tyndale martyred

1538 Henry VIII required the use of English Bibles in all churches

1545   Roman Catholic Council of Trent convened

1546   Martin Luther died; George Wishart martyred

1547   Henry VIII died and Edward VI began his reign

1549   The *Book of Common Prayer* adopted in the Church of England

1551   The *Forty-two Articles* adopted as the doctrinal statement of the Church of England

1553   Mary I began to persecute English Protestants

1555   Peace of Augsburg granted religious liberty to Lutheran princes and their subjects; Latimer, Ridley and Bradford martyred

1556   Thomas Cranmer martyred

1558   Elizabeth I crowned and restored Protestantism in England

1560   Scotland became Protestant and adopted the *Scots Confession*

1562–98   French Wars of Religion fought between Roman Catholics and Huguenots

1563   *Heidelberg Catechism* completed

1564   John Calvin died

1572   St. Bartholomew's Day Massacre; John Knox died

1584   William the Silent, Prince of Orange, assassinated

1598   Edict of Nantes granted French Huguenots a measure of religious liberty

PART ONE

FORERUNNERS
OF THE
REFORMATION

T he Reformation did not burst upon Europe like a bolt out of the blue. Just as a thunderstorm warns of its coming with dark clouds in the distance, so, too, long before Martin Luther ignited the Reformation by posting his Ninety-five Theses, brave men and women protested corruptions and false teachings in the Church of Rome and strove to bring her back to the Scriptures.

The Waldensians, living in the mountain valleys of the Alps, read the Bible in their own language and rejected the unbiblical beliefs and practices present in so much of the medieval church. Despite centuries of harsh persecution, they worshiped God and served Him according to the light of Scripture truth. Reformers before the Reformation——like Wyclif, Huss and Savonarola——sought to lead their flocks away from reliance on rituals, saints and good works and back to Christ. They called the church to return to the Word of God as the supreme authority for faith and practice——far above the pronouncements of popes and councils. And for their labors, they suffered excommunication, the confiscation of their homes and property, torture and even death by burning. But they planted the seeds that would one day spring up into the great harvest of souls for Jesus Christ known as the Protestant Reformation.

CHAPTER 1:
THE WALDENSIANS

Preservers of the True Spirit of Christianity
(1100s to the present)

Centuries before the Protestant Reformation erupted in Europe in 1517, faithful believers, living around the southern end of the Alps, clung to the Scriptures in their own language, believed its promises and sought to follow its teaching. They simply called themselves Christians, but to outsiders they were known as Waldensians——after Peter Waldo, one of their early leaders. The Waldensians loved the Word of God and memorized large portions of it, even though church leaders in their region had forbade Scripture translations in the language of the people. Believing the Bible alone was God's guide for His people; they rejected the Roman church's teachings on indulgences, purgatory, prayer to saints and other unbiblical beliefs.

The pope demanded that they stop reading or teaching the Scripture in their language and threatened them with death for heresy if they did not submit to all of the teachings of the Church of Rome. When they refused, church officials demanded that kings and princes drive them out of their lands. Through the years, the authorities burned hundreds of Waldensians at the stake along with their copies of the Scriptures. When violently driven from one place, the Waldensians quietly moved to another. Wherever they settled, they supported themselves through manual labor and farming, paid their taxes and sought to love their neighbors——earning a reputation for honesty and upright living. The Waldensians found the greatest freedom to practice their faith in remote areas, especially in the alpine valleys and mountain slopes of southeastern France and northern Italy. But even there, they were not left unmolested for long.

Their ministers taught the absolute authority and inspiration of the Bible, the sinfulness of man and the free gift of forgiveness of sins through faith in Jesus Christ. Each pastor, in his turn, served as a missionary. They went out in twos, an experienced pastor with a younger man. Clad in plain robes, they preached to the poor and read from copies of the New Testament in French or Italian. To provide for their wants and as a way to spread the gospel, the missionaries became traveling peddlers, gaining entry into cottages and castles to sell jewelry, silks and other goods. After showing their wares, customers would often ask them, "Have you nothing more to sell?"

"Yes," the Waldensians would answer, "we have jewels still more precious than anything you have seen; we would be glad to show them also. We have a precious stone, the Word of God. It is so brilliant that by its light a man may see God."

They told them about Christ's love for sinners, often leaving behind a handwritten copy of some portion of Scripture. In their wake, small pockets of believers sprang up in France, Spain, Germany, Italy, Bohemia and Poland. When church authorities discovered their activities, the missionaries often faced death by fire.

In Grenoble in 1393, one hundred fifty Waldensians——men, women and children——were burned alive together for their faith. On Christmas Day in 1400, the Waldensians in the Pragela Valley in northwestern Italy rested comfortably in their cottages, certain that the deep snow would keep their persecutors away through the winter. Suddenly, the cry, "Soldiers are coming!" shattered their peace. Grabbing their coats and hats, families fled to the mountains, carrying infants and the sick with them. Well-armed troops fell upon them and slew all who didn't make it out of the village in time. The soldiers left a few days later, after stealing valuables and supplies. Survivors found the dead lying on the ice and snow——including nearly eighty children.

In 1487, Pope Innocent VIII, determined to wipe out the Waldensians once and for all, unleashed a persecution that crashed like an avalanche upon the Waldensians living in the mountain valleys of the French and Italian Alps. The pope rallied the king of France and the dukes of Piedmont and Savoy in a crusade against them. The pope pledged to pardon anyone who waged war on the heretics for any sins they might commit during the campaign, and he promised that any man who killed a heretic would be absolved of all his past sins. Any Waldensians willing to forsake their faith and return to the Church of Rome were spared. Some gave into the pressure and declared their allegiance to the Roman church, but most remained true to Christ and His Word.

With the pope's blessing ringing in their ears, the French troops attacked the western slopes of the Alps and the forces of Piedmont and Savoy rampaged from the east. Between them, they planned to annihilate the Waldensians.

In spring 1489, French soldiers climbed the foothills and entered the Valley of Loyse, a deep gorge surrounded by towering peaks. When the people of the valley saw the great enemy host, they knew that it would be futile to stand and fight. They quickly gathered supplies and loaded them with the children and old folks into horse-drawn wagons. Climbing the steep path of the mountain slope, they sang psalms and prayed as they slogged upward. Hours later, they reached a great cave. The massive cavern formed a cathedral-size space in the side of the mountain. The men placed the women, children and the infirm in an inner hollow. Then they barricaded the cave entrance with boulders stacked chest high and stood guard.

When the soldiers arrived, they drove the defenders from the mouth of the cave. Instead of scrambling into the cavern and fighting hand-to-hand, the troops filled the entrance with twigs and branches and set it ablaze. A thick, black cloud of smoke poured into the cave. Some of the coughing Waldensians tried to fight their way out and immediately fell under the soldiers' swords. Most of the people rushed to the far end of the cave in a vain attempt to find breathable air. Afterwards, when the smoke cleared, the triumphant soldiers found the entire population of the valley——more than three thousand people——suffocated on the cave's stone floor. Never again would the praises of the Waldensians echo across the Valley of Loyse.

On the other side of the Alps, a large force of soldiers from Piedmont and Savoy under the leadership of Cataneo, the pope's representative, arrived at the foot of the mountain valleys of northwestern Italy. The Waldensians sent two representatives to plead for peace. "Do not condemn us without hearing us," they said to Cataneo. "We are Christians and faithful subjects. Our pastors are prepared to prove to you that our teachings are true to the Word of God. Beware——by persecuting us you may draw down upon yourselves the wrath of God. Remember, that if God so wills, all the forces you have assembled against us will come to nothing."

Cataneo dismissed them with a sneer, telling them that they had two choices: convert to the Roman church or die. Armed with trust in God and an intimate knowledge of the land, the Waldensians decided to fight for their lives. They abandoned dozens of their villages, hastily packed some meager supplies and hiked into the Valley of Angrogna in the heart of the mountains. Further in, where the valley narrows, the Waldensians prepared to defend themselves. After they moved the women and children to the rear of the valley, the men sharpened their pikes, spears and arrows.

When the soldiers arrived, they rained a torrent of arrows on the Waldensians who covered themselves with their shields made of deerskin and tree bark. The Waldensians cried out in prayer, "O God of our fathers, help us! O God, deliver us!" The lead captain heard their prayer, raised the visor of his metal helmet and shouted back, "My warriors will give you God's answer!" No sooner had the words left his mouth, when an arrow struck him between the eyes, and he fell down dead. The loss of their leader caused the soldiers to hesitate, and some started to fall back. Then the Waldensians fired a burst of arrows and charged. They chased the army back down the valley and cut down many of them. By nightfall, the men had returned to the women and children, and they celebrated the victory with songs of praise to their Savior. The next morning, they braced for a second attack that they knew would be more determined than the first.

Cataneo, embarrassed and enraged that his men had been driven off by herdsmen and farmers, regrouped his forces and marched back up the valley. When they reached the place of the previous battle, their prey was nowhere to be found. They pressed forward through the narrowing canyon until they reached a long gorge. The only way through was a cramped rocky ledge with a mountain wall on one side and a sheer cliff——falling hundreds of meters to the canyon floor——on the other. Carefully placing their steps, the soldiers advanced. Suddenly, a heavy fog like a great black robe dropped from the peaks above and cloaked the gorge in darkness. Cataneo's soldiers could barely see the man in front of them——unable to advance or retreat.

Just then, the Waldensian fighters, hiding on a ridge above the soldiers, sprang into action. They rolled down boulders and hurled stones upon their enemy, crushing some and sweeping others off the cliff. A detachment of Waldensians with swords drawn attacked the soldiers from the front. Overcome with fear and confusion, the troops turned to flee. As they struggled to retreat, they jostled one another off the edge. Far more perished in their desperate attempt to escape than fell under the blows of the Waldensians. Few of the invaders made it out of the valley alive.

Not long after, fresh troops arrived and intermittently attacked the Waldensians for nearly a year. The troops slaughtered any Waldensians they captured. They stole what they could carry and torched everything else——homes, churches, barns and fields. But hundreds of soldiers perished at the hands of the Waldensians. Finally, the young Duke of Savoy called for a truce and a meeting with Waldensian leaders. The duke had reluctantly lent his support to the pope's crusade against them. When he met with the representatives of the mountain people, he marveled at their sturdy faith and righteous lives. "I did not know," he said, "that I had so virtuous, so faithful and so obedient subjects as the Waldensians. I had been told that you were one-eyed monsters with four rows of sharp black teeth."

The duke apologized for the suffering inflicted upon them by his men, and pledged that from that day forward, they could live in their mountain valleys in peace. And so the Waldensians enjoyed a reprieve from persecution for a time.

About forty years later, when the Reformation took root in Germany and Switzerland, the Waldensians heard that tens of thousands of people trusted in God's grace in Christ and looked to the Scriptures as their only rule of faith and life. They sent a delegation of pastors to see for themselves. In 1530, some went to Neuchatel and met with William Farel, and others traveled to Strasbourg to confer with Martin Bucer. Two went to Basel and explained to Oecolampadius their teachings and practices. "Sir," they said, "tell us if you approve of our beliefs. And if you discover any errors, teach us the right way from the Word of God."

Oecolampadius embraced these believers who had preserved so much of the true faith in Christ despite generations of persecution. "We give thanks to our most gracious Father," Oecolampadius told them, "that He has called you to such marvelous light, during ages when thick darkness covered almost the whole world under the empire of the Antichrist. We love you as brothers!"

The Swiss reformers sent Christian books and Bibles to the Waldensians. Their ministers conferred together and prayed for one another. After living for so long in isolation, the Christians of the Alps rejoiced to be a part of the rapidly-growing and renewed Church of Jesus Christ. One church historian summed up the centuries-long experience of the Waldensians, saying, "They always carried along with them the true spirit of Christianity."

CHAPTER 2:
JOHN WYCLIF
AND THE LOLLARDS

*The Evangelical Doctor and the Poor Preachers
(Wyclif c.1330–1384, Lollards 1370s–mid 1500s)*

For years, John Wyclif, the leading theologian of Oxford University, had rankled the pope and the bishops of England. Wyclif's teachings came out of his study of the Bible. He taught that sinners are forgiven only through the grace of God by believing in Christ. Indulgences, masses and pilgrimages do not add to salvation, he said——only faith in Christ saves. "There is no merit in us," Wyclif preached. "For according to God's teaching, we are all sinners from our birth so that we cannot so much as think a good thought or perform a good work unless Jesus sends it. His mercy comes to us, follows us, helps us and keeps us in grace. So then it is not good for us to trust in our merits, in our virtues or in our righteousness. It is only good to trust in God."

Wyclif argued that the bread and wine of the Lord's Supper are not the physical body and blood of Jesus as the Roman church taught, but are signs and seals of Christ's spiritual presence with His children. Wyclif's advice to the English king and Parliament not to pay papal taxes angered church leaders for it would deprive the Church of Rome treasure that they had bilked from England for hundreds of years. "God entrusted the flock to the pope to feed and not to fleece," Wyclif said.

He taught that the Bible alone is sufficient to guide the church, not the teachings of popes, councils or kings that are contrary to Scripture. And he believed that God meant the Scriptures for everyone. "Jesus taught the people simply and in their own language," Wyclif said. "At Pentecost, the Holy Spirit gave the apostles the gift of tongues so that everyone could hear the good news in his own language."

Enraged by Wyclif's ideas, Pope Gregory XI demanded that the king of England and the archbishop of Canterbury do something about him. "John Wyclif," the pope wrote, "is vomiting out of the filthy dungeon of his heart most wicked and damnable heresies. He hopes to deceive the faithful and lead them to the edge of destruction." The pope insisted that Wyclif be tried for heresy and burned to death. But when Pope Gregory died suddenly, a great struggle ensued over who should be his successor——a struggle which enabled Wyclif to continue preaching, teaching, writing and training young men to preach the Word of God. Students came to Oxford from all over Europe to learn from Wyclif, the "Evangelical doctor," as students called him. Many returned to their homelands to preach about Jesus Christ to their countrymen.

Wyclif made translating the Scriptures into English his highest priority. The short and frail Wyclif, with the help of two trusted co-workers, toiled day and night to translate the Bible. "Press on in this work," he told his helpers, "for if the people of England will read the Scriptures for themselves it will be the surest road for them to follow Christ and come to heaven." After eleven years of labor, they translated into English all of the Old and New Testaments. In those days before the printing press, Wyclif recruited scores of Oxford students to make handwritten copies of the Scriptures.

At that time in England, church officials banned translating and distributing the Scriptures in the common language of the people. They did not want the people studying the Bible for themselves for fear that the clergy would lose influence and the unity of the Church of Rome would be broken. Violating unbiblical church laws did not trouble Wyclif. "The pope's words should be followed only so far as he follows the words of Christ," he said. "I am ready to follow the teachings of Scripture even unto death if necessary."

Wyclif sent out hundreds of young men that he called "poor preachers" dressed in simple brown robes with handwritten copies of the English Bible. They traveled across Britain proclaiming the good news of Christ and singing songs of praise. "After your sermon is ended," Wyclif told his traveling preachers, "visit the sick, the aged, the poor, the blind, and the lame and help them as you are able."

Village by village they preached and read from the Scriptures in churchyards, cottages, town squares and fields. The Lollards, the name given to Wyclif's followers, led thousands of men, women and children to faith in Jesus Christ, and these new believers began to learn the Word of God for the first time in their lives.

The archbishop of Canterbury ordered English churchmen to stop the Lollards, and he urged the king to root them out of the land. "If we permit these heretics to continue," he told the king, "our destruction is inevitable. We must silence these Lollards——these psalm-singers."

Local priests harassed the evangelists and fell upon them when they entered a town. But the people often sided with the preachers, forming a strong ring around them to protect them from harm.

In 1382, the archbishop convened a church court at Oxford and summoned Wyclif, whose health was failing, to stand before it. Wyclif faced his accusers, rebuking them for not following the Word of God and for using church office for selfish gain. The court banished Wyclif from Oxford University. They wanted to have him burned for heresy, but some of his supporters in Parliament prevented it. So he returned to his parish church in Lutterworth and labored on. "I intend with my whole heart," he said, "by the grace of God, to be a true Christian and as long as breath remains in me to proclaim and defend the law of Christ."

Two years later, Wyclif died of a stroke, but his followers carried on the work. Church leaders, determined to crush the Lollards, ordered all copies of the English Bible and the writings of Wyclif burned. People faced fines, imprisonment and even execution for sharing Wyclif's ideas or owning his writings. Many Lollards met a fiery death for spreading the good news of full forgiveness in Christ and for reading the Scriptures in English. Some died in the flames with scraps of English Scripture tied to their necks by their tormentors.

This fierce persecution failed to snuff out the Lollard's gospel light. So many people accepted Wyclif's teachings that one English churchman complained, "If you meet two people on the road, you can be sure that one is a disciple of Wyclif."

John Oldcastle, an outspoken Lollard and a prominent nobleman and member of the House of Lords, came to a living faith in Christ through the preaching of John Wyclif. He used his wealth to pay for hand-copying of Wyclif's writings and the Scriptures in English. Oldcastle supported many preachers who traveled the country proclaiming Christ and giving away portions of the Scriptures.

Oldcastle's activities inflamed the wrath of church leaders who warned the king, "Oldcastle is a heretic, a troubler of the peace and an enemy of the realm." They hauled him before a church court held in a monastery near St. Paul's Cathedral in London. Churchmen and the common people turned out to see the trial of the famous nobleman. "Heretic," a priest said, "do you believe in the pronouncements of the church?"

"I believe in the Scriptures and all that is found in them," Oldcastle answered, "but not in your idle pronouncements."

"You follow that heretic Wyclif!" one churchman shouted.

"Before I knew Wyclif," Oldcastle replied, "I never tried to resist sin. But after I knew that virtuous man whom you disdain, I learned to fear my Lord God, and I saw my errors and turned away from them. I never knew that I could find so much grace when I followed your instructions."

At times, the crowd had difficulty hearing Oldcastle over the jeers of the priests and friars. The churchmen demanded that he recant his errors and yield to the authority of the church. "My belief is that all the Scriptures of the sacred book are true. All that is grounded upon them, I believe thoroughly, for I know it is God's pleasure that I should do so. But in your laws and idle determinations, I have no belief. For your deeds show that you stand against Christ and are obstinately set against His holy law and will."

They threatened to condemn him to death as a heretic if he did not recant. "My faith is fixed," he said, "do with me what you please."

After the death sentence was pronounced, Oldcastle said, "You may condemn my body, but my soul you cannot hurt."

Oldcastle turned to the assembled crowd and told them, "Good people, I am not condemned for breaking God's commandments. It is to protect their own laws and traditions that I and other men are so cruelly treated."

Guards cast him into the Tower of London. He escaped for a time, and tried to organize a revolt against the king's government. In 1417, he was captured. An executioner hung him upon the gallows with a chain and lit a fire under him where he slowly roasted to death. Spectators reported that he cheerfully accepted his death and prayed that God would forgive his persecutors.

Anne of Bohemia*, the wife of King Richard II, embraced Wyclif's teachings. When she died in 1394, the Bohemian members of her court returned home and brought Wyclif's writings with them. His ideas found fertile ground among the Czech people. The Czech preachers, John Huss and Jerome of Prague, suffered death by burning for preaching the truths of Scripture and exposing the false teachings of the Church of Rome. Czech missionaries went out to preach the good news throughout Europe. In 1433, a Czech named Paul Craw was burned at the stake in St. Andrews, Scotland, for teaching the ideas of Wyclif and Huss. The authorities so feared his preaching that they ordered a brass ball stuffed into his mouth to prevent him from speaking at the stake.

Many Lollard women paid the ultimate price for their faith. Joan Brownton, an eighty-year-old grandmother, died at the stake when she would not renounce her Lollard faith. A woman from Leith, Scotland, suffered imprisonment when she prayed to Christ for help during the pains of childbirth instead of the Virgin Mary. In 1519, the authorities in Coventry, England, arrested Mrs. Smith*, a widowed mother who worshiped secretly with other Lollards in the city, for reading to her children from the Gospel of Luke and teaching them to recite the Lord's Prayer and the Ten Commandments in English. "If you recant," the bishop of Coventry told her, "you may

---

* Read about Anne of Bohemia, Mrs. Smith, and other Christian heroines in Richard M. Hannula's *Radiant: Fifty Remarkable Women in Church History* (2015).

return home." She refused. A few days later, guards led Mrs. Smith and six Lollard fathers to an open space in the center of Coventry. They tied them to a stake and burned them to death for the crime of teaching their children the Scriptures in English.

When the Protestant Reformation swept across Europe in the first half of the sixteenth century, the Lollards rejoiced that the Word of God was being restored to its proper place in many parts of the Christian church.

REFORMATION BASICS 1

Solo Christo ("Through Christ Alone")

The Scriptures make clear that salvation is through Christ alone (*solo Christo* in Latin). "For there is one God, and there is one mediator between God and men, the man Christ Jesus" (1 Tim. 2:5).

But the Roman church taught the people to pray to Mary and the saints in heaven to seek their intercession with God. By the late Middle Ages, most churchgoers prayed more to Mary and the saints than they did to God. As the reformers read the Scriptures, they did not find prayer to saints or Mary. They learned that it is only through faith in Christ and His death on the cross that sinners find forgiveness and are restored to a right relationship with God. So the reformers called their hearers to look to Christ as their only mediator before God. When asked if Christians should pray to saints, Olaf Petri the Swedish reformer answered, "Do not put your trust in any human being, such as the Virgin Mary or any other saint, but trust in God alone."

John Calvin wrote, "In regard to the saints…the Scripture calls us away from all others to Christ alone, since our heavenly Father is pleased to gather together all things in him, it were the extreme of stupidity, not to say madness, to attempt to obtain access by means of others, so as to be drawn away from him without whom access [to God] cannot be obtained."

CHAPTER 3:
JOHN HUSS

Bohemian Reformer and Martyr
(1369–1415)

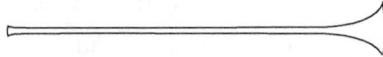

On October 2, 1412, the priests of Prague, Bohemia, finally possessed what they had long petitioned the pope and the king to provide: an order to seize John Huss, forbid his preaching, excommunicate him and destroy Bethlehem Chapel. The leading theologian and preacher of Prague, John Huss, had been a thorn in the side of the priests for years. His church, Bethlehem Chapel, overflowed with people for its services. Huss conducted worship in Czech, the language of the people, and not Latin as decreed by the pope. He preached the Word of God and condemned laziness and greed in the clergy. Now, with the prodding of the priests and some leading men of the city, a large crowd assembled outside the senate house.

"Come on, men," their leader shouted, "we'll march to Bethle-hem Chapel; arrest that heretic Huss and level the building to the ground." The people of Bethlehem Chapel rallied to the defense of their pastor and church.

"Brothers and sisters," Huss told them, "they want to block God's Holy Word and tear down a chapel built for His service." The friends of Huss met the mob with such determination that the an-gry townsmen left without Huss and without harming the chapel. But his enemies kept up the attack. The pope placed all of Prague under interdict, forbidding any church services until authorities ar-rested Huss. The city was divided between supporters of Huss and supporters of the pope. Tensions mounted, and even fights broke out. John Huss did not obey the pope's ban but continued to preach that all who trust in Christ are fully forgiven and have peace with God. "Christ commanded His disciples to go into all the world and preach," he said. "No pope can stop what Christ taught to be done."

Although expelled from Prague by the king of Bohemia, huge crowds flocked to hear him speak in fields, forests, villages and cas-tles. He stayed in touch with his congregation by sending letters and sometimes sneaking into the city to visit them. "My greatest comfort," he wrote them, "is to see you earnestly following the Bi-ble. Please pray that the Word of God may not be kept back in me." Some of his friends, worried for his safety, asked whether he could give in to the pope but a little. "I will confess Christ as long as He gives me grace to do so," Huss said. "I will resist to the death all agreement with falsehood. A good death is better than a bad life."

For two years he wrote, preached and resisted the ban of the pope while growing numbers of Czechs sided with Huss. As the un-rest grew, the German Emperor Sigismund feared it would spread into his empire. So he encouraged the king of Bohemia to send

Huss to appear before the church council meeting in the Swiss city of Constance. The emperor promised Huss protection from harm, giving him a letter of safe conduct to and from Constance. Huss gladly agreed to go because he longed to defend his teachings before the council. "Under the safe conduct of your protection," he wrote the emperor, "I shall appear before the council. I hope that I shall not be afraid to confess the Lord Christ and, if need be, to die for the truth of His Law."

Many in Huss's congregation warned him not to trust the emperor's safe conduct. One man, eyes brimming with tears, gently took his hand and said, "God be with you; I am afraid you will not return again unharmed. Dearest Master John, may the King of Heaven reward you for the good and true instruction that I received from you."

Huss bid farewell to his flock saying, "Remember, Christ suffered for the sake of His chosen. If my death can glorify His name, then may He give me grace to endure with good courage whatever evil may befall me. May the Lord watch over you and bring you into eternal peace and glory." With two knights armed for battle riding beside him for protection, he set out for Constance. For three weeks he traveled across Germany to Switzerland. Wherever he went, he left behind a handwritten copy of the Ten Commandments, for the people knew next to nothing of the Bible.

Not long after his arrival and despite the emperor's promise of protection, soldiers arrested him and threw him into a putrid dungeon cell next to an open sewer. The stench and foul air ruined his health, giving him severe headaches and throwing him into vomiting fits. Though deprived of his books and Bible, ill and nearly starved and chained day and night, he prepared his defense. But the council had no intention of letting Huss explain himself, deciding in advance that he could either recant or be burned. Huss requested an advocate to speak on his behalf.

"We do not grant such privileges to heretics," they told him.

"Well, then," Huss said, "let the Lord Jesus be my advocate, who also will soon be your judge." Finally, after months of imprisonment, suffering from headaches and stomach pains, Huss was brought to the cathedral before the council to hear the charges against him. They sat him on a tall wooden stool in the middle of the cathedral, where he was surrounded by princes, bishops, cardinals and theologians. Emperor Sigismund sat on a throne. The smell of incense lingered from the high mass celebrated before his arrival. A stack of books and papers were laid on the table before him. "These are your writings. Will you admit they are full of false teachings?" they asked.

"I am ready to retract anything in them," Huss said, "if I am shown from Holy Scripture where I am in error." A councilman came forward and picked up one of the books. "Burn it!" shouted several men in the assembly. The councilman called for quiet and then read aloud a short chapter. "Do you retract this?" he asked. As Huss attempted to quote passages from the Bible and the writings of the church fathers to defend the chapter, a loud howling like wolves erupted from the council. "Away with your arguments," they shouted, "Say yes or no."

Each time he tried to speak, they interrupted him with howls. When he managed to say that Christ alone and not the pope was the head of the church, the councilmen shook their heads and laughed.

They called on him once more to accept the judgment of the council and recant. "It would be better for me," Huss said, "that a millstone was hung around my neck and that I should be cast into the sea before I should deny the truths of God."

Soon the judgment was read: "The holy council, having only God before its eye, condemns John Huss to be a stubborn and open heretic."

"I never was stubborn," Huss said. "I only demand that you show me from Scripture where I have erred." Huss looked to the emperor who had promised him protection. The emperor's cheeks flushed red; he turned his head and said nothing. Falling to his knees, Huss prayed aloud, "O Christ, the council has condemned your Word. Lord Jesus, forgive my enemies; as you know I have been falsely accused by them. Forgive them for the sake of Your great mercy."

A roar of laughter pealed from the councilmen who pointed at Huss and mimicked his prayer. The council turned him over to the secular rulers who condemned him to death by fire. Before he was executed, six bishops wrapped priestly robes around his shoulders and placed a eucharistic cup in his hands. Then they stripped him of his robes, saying he was no longer a minister in Christ's church. Snatching the cup from him, one said, "We take from you, condemned Judas, the cup of salvation."

"But I trust in God," Huss replied, "that today I shall drink of the cup of salvation with my Lord Jesus Christ in His kingdom." While cursing him, they set on his head a hat painted with devils and the word "arch-heretic." "My Lord Jesus," Huss said, "wore a crown of thorns for me; why should I not be willing, for His sake, to wear this."

A bishop called out, "Now we give over your soul to the devil."

Huss looked to heaven and said, "And I commit my soul to Jesus." A guard of a thousand armed men led Huss through the city, holding back the people who thronged the streets. A large crowd followed close behind to the place of execution. Huss dropped to his knees and with tears in his eyes prayed lines from the Psalms and said, "Into Your hands, Lord, I commit my spirit. Lord, help me to endure this cruel and shameful death for preaching Your holy gospel." With an old chain, brown and flaking, they bound his hands behind his back and strapped his neck to the stake. "My Lord Jesus," he said, "was bound with a harder chain than this for my sake, and why then should I be ashamed of this rusty one?"

As they piled wood and straw around him to his neck, a nobleman called out, "There is still time. Recant."

"What error," Huss answered, "should I recant? I shall die with joy today in the faith of the gospel of Jesus Christ which I have preached." When the fire was lit, he sang out with a loud voice, "Jesus, Son of the living God, have mercy on me." They threw his clothes and shoes into the flames and later scooped up the ashes, casting them into the Rhine River.

His death inspired tens of thousands of his countrymen to boldly follow Christ. And one hundred years later, his stand on the Word of God encouraged Martin Luther and the other reformers in their belief that Scripture is the supreme standard for what Christians are to believe and do. Luther praised Huss's courage and faithfulness. "If he is to be regarded as a heretic," Luther wrote, "then no person under the sun can be looked upon as a true Christian."

"John Huss: Bohemian Reformer and Martyr" is excerpted from Richard M. Hannula's *Trial and Triumph: Stories from Church History* (1999).

CHAPTER 4:
GIROLAMO SAVONAROLA

Preacher of Righteousness

(1452–1498)

In the spring of 1492, Lorenzo de Medici, the dictator of Florence, Italy, lay on his deathbed. Lorenzo the Magnificent did not seem so magnificent now. His sumptuous palace——buzzing with servants and filled with the finest artwork——could do nothing for his shriveled body, wasting away from disease. He found no comfort in the priests who, despite his brutality, had always assured him of salvation. Now his sins loomed ominously before him, and he feared the fast-approaching judgment of God. Then he remembered Savonarola, the preaching monk. Savonarola had never flattered him and spoke the stark truth no matter the consequences. "I know no honest friar but him," Lorenzo told an aide. "Send for him."

Medici, like all the followers of the Church of Rome, believed that in order to receive forgiveness from God, a repentant sinner must confess his sins to a priest. The priest would give the penitent something to do as a sign of his repentance and absolve his sins on behalf of God, saying, "I absolve you from your sins in the name of the Father and of the Son and of the Holy Spirit." Lorenzo longed to hear those words from the lips of Savonarola.

Savonarola arrived at the palace wearing his threadbare robe, his dark complexion and large nose partially hidden under his cowl. "Father," Lorenzo said, his voice quaking, "I want to confess my sins and receive absolution." Through his tears, he confessed that he had shed innocent blood and extorted large sums of money. As he spoke, Lorenzo grew so overcome with grief that he could barely utter a word. "God is good, God is merciful," Savonarola reminded him. When Lorenzo finished speaking, Savonarola looked long into his eyes, raised his right hand and said, "For me to pronounce absolution, you need to do three things."

"What things, Father?" asked Lorenzo.

"You must have a full and living faith in God's mercy."

"I do," he answered.

"And you must restore all the wealth that you unjustly took from others, or charge your sons to restore it in your name." Lorenzo's face fell at this requirement. After mulling it over for a few minutes, he weakly nodded his head.

"Lastly," Savonarola said, standing over the dying prince, "you must restore liberty to the people of Florence."

Lorenzo clenched his jaw and glared at him. He had spent his life consolidating his power at the expense of the people's freedom. His will was law. The power of the Medici family was one thing he would never give up. Mustering all his strength, he rolled on his side, turning his back on the monk. Savonarola left without giving him absolution. Not long after, Lorenzo died.

From the moment that Savonarola had arrived three years earlier at San Marco——the Dominican monastery in the heart of Florence—— his faithful preaching and forthright truth-telling clashed with Lorenzo and his court. Florence, a wealthy commercial center, embraced the Renaissance and its devotion to art and learning. Lorenzo was a popular despot who won the people's favor by sponsoring great public feasts and carnivals that featured wine, song and debauchery. The citizens loved to hear the stories of classical Greece and reenact their pagan revelries. Savonarola spoke out against it. "Those ancient authors whom they praise are strangers to Christ and the Christian virtues," he preached, "and their art is idolatry of heathen gods."

Most priests, monks and bishops followed the trend. They quoted the Greek philosophers in their sermons, but failed to proclaim the Scripture. "The preachers preach to please princes and to be praised by them," Savonarola said. "Instead of teaching so many other books, why don't they expound the one book in which is the law and spirit of life——the Gospel!"

At first, Savonarola preached to his fellow monks and the few people who came to the monastery church. He spoke simply in Italian, not Latin, so the people could understand him as he taught the law of God and the sacrifice of Christ. "Flee from your sins," he preached. "Behold there will come a time of darkness, when Christ will rain fire and storm upon the wicked. Fly from your sins and turn to Christ." They had never heard anything like it before. "I felt a cold shiver run through me, and my hair stand on end," one man said about the effect of his preaching.

Soon the church at San Marco overflowed with all who came to hear him. To accommodate the large crowds, he started preaching in the Duomo, the grand cathedral of Florence. There, he preached to the rich and the poor——to over ten thousand people at once—— including Lorenzo and his officials and the bishops and their clerics. They were used to bland sermons that did not call them to repent. Shunning church tradition and the teachings of men, Savonarola preached from the Word of God. "I take the Scriptures as my only guide," he said.

He sought to shake his hearers out of their sins and drive them to Christ by proclaiming the wrath of God against wickedness. "This city shall no longer be called Florence, but a den of thieves, wickedness and bloodshed!" he preached. "Repent, for the Lord will have mercy on the just." People wept and cried out as they imagined the com- ing judgment of the Lord. Then Savonarola pointed them to Christ. "Love led Christ to the cross," he said, "love raised Him from the dead and made Him ascend into heaven to accomplish our redemption."

Savonarola saved his sternest words for the wealthy and power- ful. "Consider well, O you rich, for affliction shall smite you," he proclaimed. "Arise, O Lord and deliver Your church from the hands of tyrants and from the hands of sinful bishops."

His preaching ignited fierce opposition from the leaders of church and state. They called him "the chattering friar," and they plotted to get rid of him. After Lorenzo died, his son Piero banished Savonarola from Florence. However, at that time, the king of France and his army had invaded Italy, conquering one city after another. Savonarola believed that God was using the French to punish the Italians for their sins and to purify the church. When Piero——in an effort to preserve Florence from destruction——handed over the city's fortresses to the French king and paid him a large ransom, the people turned against him. Piero fled. Soon, the people chafed under the rough occupation of the French troops. They looked to

Savonarola for leadership. He met the French king and said, "The people are afflicted by your stay in Florence, and you waste your time. God has called you to renew His church. Go forth to your high calling lest God visit you with His wrath and choose another instrument in your stead to carry out His plans!" With the promise that Florence would not aid France's enemies, the king withdrew his forces from the city.

With the Medici and the French army gone, Savonarola urged the city council and the people to create a new republic——one that would honor God. He warned them against allowing one man to control the state as the Medici had done. "Jesus Christ seeks to become your king!" he said. Raising a crucifix in his hand, he asked, "Florence, will you have Him to be your king?" With tears in their eyes, many stood up and cried out, "Long live Christ, our king!"

"Citizens, would you be free?" he said in a sermon. "First of all, love God, love your neighbor and love one another. If you have this loving union among you, true liberty will be yours."

Savonarola called the people to lay aside immorality and rid themselves of anything that tempted them to sin. On a February evening in 1496, the people threw their immoral books, lewd pictures, gambling cards and other stumbling blocks to holiness into a great bonfire in the central piazza. "Pious hymns took the place of crude carnival songs," one man reported. "The townsfolk passed their leisure hours reading the Bible or Savonarola's works. All prayed frequently, flocked to the churches and gave generously to the poor."

While many people in Florence repented, the bishops and councilmen resented his influence and plotted to get rid of him. When the pope excommunicated Savonarola, he ignored it. He pointed out that the pope was a notorious sinner who had bought his office with a bribe. "The church is teeming with abomination from the crown of her head to the soles of her feet," he said.

Before long, the city council banned Savonarola from the pulpit. At first he complied, but then he felt God's call to resume preaching. In May 1497, he announced that he would ignore the ban and preach again in the Duomo. His supporters warned him of the danger. "I'm ready to lay down my life for my office," he replied.

His enemies filled the Duomo's pulpit with garbage and nailed spikes into it. This did not keep him from preaching. But over time, more and more people grew weary of Savonarola's calls to repent and live holy lives, and they turned against him. Savonarola's enemies whipped up a mob and sent them with a band of soldiers to capture him from San Marco. The friars barred the gates to protect him. When the besiegers began to batter the monastery walls with cannon, the friars fought back, even though Savonarola told them not to. As violence raged outside, Savonarola preached a final sermon to a small crowd in the chapel. "Have courage, embrace the cross, and you will find the port of salvation," he said.

The siege ended when Savonarola and two other monks turned themselves over to the attackers. In order to force a confession out of Savonarola, they stretched him on the rack, straining his muscles and making every limb quiver with pain. For nearly two weeks, they tormented him. Eventually, they broke his will, and he signed a confession. But the pope in Rome thought his written confession inadequate. "Try again," the pope commanded the authorities in Florence. "We've had to deal with a man of most extraordinary patience and suffering," they told the pope. "Even with the help of torture, we can scarcely pull anything out of him."

For the next month, Savonarola endured another round of torture applied by agents of the pope, and he waited patiently for his execution. In his cell, he wrote about his faith in Christ. Friends smuggled the writings out of jail and had them printed. The *Prison Meditations* revealed his growing trust in the grace of God. "Do you have faith?" he asked himself. "Yes: this is a great grace of God, for faith is His gift, not of your works, that no one may glory in them."

On May 23, 1498, guards led Savonarola and his two friends to a tall scaffold in the central piazza. Church officials stripped the condemned monks of their priestly robes, scraped their hands raw and shaved their heads——symbolically wiping away their ordination.

A bishop stepped forward and declared, "I separate you from the church militant and triumphant!" "You have no power to separate me from the church triumphant to which I go," Savonarola replied. After the hangman did his work, guards lit a large pile of wood and straw, and they burned the bodies of the three martyrs.

Savonarola's ideas did not die with him. His books and printed sermons continued to be read widely in Italy and beyond, even though the Church of Rome banned them as heresy. Martin Luther, the great reformer of Germany, thought so highly of Savonarola's *Prison Meditations* that he had the booklet reprinted in Wittenberg. "Although some theological mud still adhered to the feet of that holy man," Luther wrote of Savonarola, "nevertheless, he maintained justification by faith alone without works."

Girolamo Savonarola's life and preaching helped to pave the way for the good news of Christ to be fully recovered by the reformers who followed him.

COMPREHENSION QUESTIONS

for Introduction, Overview, and Part One

1. List several unbiblical beliefs and practices implemented by the Church of Rome during the Middle Ages.

2. What developments helped to make Europe ripe for the Reformation in the early sixteenth century?

3. Which monarchs in Western Europe were the greatest enemies of the Reformation?

4. Which monarchs in Western Europe used their power to support the Reformation?

5. In what ways were the Waldensians forerunners of the Reformation?

6. Why is John Wyclif considered the most important reformer before the age of the Reformation?

7. Why was Wyclif not burned at the stake for his views?

8. Why was John Huss burned at the stake at the Council of Constance?

9. Why did Savonarola clash with Lorenzo de Medici?

10. Why was Savonarola burned at the stake?

PART TWO

THE REFORMATION IN GERMANY, SWEDEN AND THE NETHERLANDS

A t the start of the sixteenth century, nearly everyone agreed that the Church of Rome stood in desperate need of reform. Heart-felt worship that engaged the congregation had been replaced by an elaborate ritual performed by a priest in Latin, a language that the people did not understand. Many immoral and corrupt churchmen from monks to the pope lived for worldly pleasure and set miserable examples for the flock. The sale of church offices and the sale of indulgences——the pope's promise to reduce punishment in purgatory——made the church look more like a business than a ministry. When a German monk named Martin Luther protested against indulgences, he ignited a wildfire of change. Printing presses made possible the wide distribution of Scripture translations and the writings of Luther and other reformers in many languages. The good news of full forgiveness in Jesus Christ found fertile soil in the hearts of monks and priests, nobles and commoners across Europe. Despite fierce resistance from church authorities, a growing number of voices called for reforms in the teachings and practices of the church.

If Luther had lived in the Netherlands or Spain, he would have been burned at the stake for his ideas, but, in the providence of God, his home was Saxony, an important German principality that enjoyed a measure of independence in the empire. The ruler of Saxony, Frederick the Wise, chose to protect Luther when the pope and Emperor Charles V declared him a heretic and demanded that he be delivered over for punishment. However, Charles V wielded his unrestricted power in Spain and the Netherlands to crush followers of the Reformation. Hundreds of Spanish and Dutch Evangelicals perished at the stake, and thousands more fled their homes to escape the relentless persecution. Although Protestants were largely extinguished from Spain and Italy, their numbers grew in the

Netherlands despite violent attacks against them. Eventually, Dutch Evangelicals rose up and resisted the brutality of the emperor's forces, and they won their freedom to worship God according to the Scriptures. In Sweden, Evangelicals trained by Luther brought the gospel of grace to their homeland. When King Gustavus embraced the Reformation, Sweden quickly became a Protestant nation.

CHAPTER 5:
MARTIN LUTHER

Father of the Reformation
(1483–1546)

On a late summer day in 1517, the sun cast a golden glow over a German town near the border of Saxony. A great assembly of peasants, merchants, lords and ladies waited in eager expectation. Trumpet blasts announced the approach of a grand procession making its way to the town square. At the head of the parade strode the mayor, and then marched the priests, monks and friars hoisting brilliant banners of red, white and purple emblazoned with the cross of Christ and the golden keys, symbolizing the power of the pope. The traveling preacher, dressed in a white robe, rode in an ornate carriage. At the end came a churchman lifting high a gold embroidered velvet cushion upon which rested a great parchment, the pope's Bull of Indulgence——a papal letter offering forgiveness. As the banners were set in place around a platform in the square, the murmuring of the crowd died down and the preacher named Tetzel rose to speak.

"Take care to listen, dear children, for God and St. Peter are calling you," he said, pointing his finger and making eye contact with people in every corner of the square. "Do you know that your life is like a small ship caught in a terrible storm? Sin and temptation toss you about. Are you ever going to make it to the safety of heaven?"

Downcast eyes revealed to Tetzel that his message was hitting the mark. "Today is the day," he continued, "and this is the hour to have all your sins removed, for the Holy Father, Pope Leo, has declared a special indulgence. Confess your sins, drop some money in the box, and you will be forgiven."

Tetzel preyed on their fear of purgatory, a place which the Roman church taught existed between heaven and hell where Christians after death were punished for their sins and purified for heaven. "And, my children," Tetzel added, "do not forget your dear dead relatives. Listen, can't you hear them calling to you from the pains of purgatory? 'Pity us! Pity us! We are in terrible torment, but you can free us for a pittance. Will you not drop a few coins into the box and open the door of heaven to us?'" He closed his appeal shouting, "As soon as the coin in the coffer rings, the soul from purgatory springs!"

Many people rushed forward, emptied their pockets and returned home with joy, clutching to their breasts the letters of indulgence. Some from Wittenberg excitedly told their priest, Martin Luther, about Tetzel's message and showed him their indulgences. Thirty-four-year-old Martin Luther, the crown of his head shaved as a sign of his monastic order, frowned and sighed deeply. Luther used to buy indulgences, too. But his study of the Scriptures had led him to question many of the teachings of the Church of Rome. He knew God's forgiveness could not be bought, and he no longer believed that the pope had the power to forgive sins or remit punishments in purgatory.

However, his congregation, ignorant of the Scriptures, accepted without question the Roman church's teachings. They believed that they could win God's favor through indulgences, prayers to saints and the veneration of relics——bits of bones, hair and teeth supposedly from the bodies of dead saints.

The Castle Church in Wittenberg housed more than 17,000 relics——the largest collection in Germany——claiming among them four strands of the Virgin Mary's hair, a piece of straw from the baby Jesus' manger, a nail from the cross and a piece of bread from the Last Supper. The pope decreed that visitors to the Castle Church on All Saints Day who venerated the relics and gave a contribution could reduce their time in purgatory by over one million years!

Luther yearned to lead the people out of the darkness of superstition and vain works and into the light of faith in Jesus Christ. The thought of Tetzel's jingle "As soon as the coin in the coffer rings, the soul from purgatory springs," emboldened him to act. Martin Luther publicly declared Tetzel's teaching and the sale of indulgences a sham.

"Christ alone can forgive sins," he proclaimed. "The pope has no power to forgive or to free souls from purgatory. If he had such power, why does he not release everyone from purgatory at once? Why does he not do it free of charge?"

Then Luther wrote a list of ninety-five arguments or theses against indulgences. On October 31, 1517, he nailed the Ninety-five Theses to the door of the Castle Church, challenging church leaders and scholars to debate the sale of indulgences. A printer published the theses, and soon they spread throughout Germany and beyond. What Luther had intended to be a discussion on indulgences among the university professors and churchmen of Wittenberg exploded into a spiritual struggle that engulfed all of Europe.

Martin Luther had been engaged in a desperate search to find God's forgiveness for years. He had painstakingly performed every duty recommended by the church, but his sin and guilt continued to overwhelm him. Then, in the months following the posting of the Ninety-five Theses, while studying the Scripture, he read Romans 1:17, "For in the gospel a righteousness from God is revealed, a righteousness that is by faith from first to last, just as it is written: 'The righteous will live by faith.'"

The truth of God revealed in that verse transformed Luther's life. He discovered that a sinner is not made right with God by anything he does himself but only by trusting in what Christ has done for him. "I felt that I was reborn and had gone through open doors to paradise," he said. "I saw that God had given me the righteousness of Christ through faith. Christ suffered all the penalty for my sin on the cross. By faith Christ's righteousness becomes my righteousness." This good news liberated Luther from striving to win God's grace through pilgrimages, indulgences and good works. His service to God now flowed out of gratitude for his salvation.

Luther began preaching that sinners are declared righteous in God's sight only through faith in Christ. "He is not justified who does many works," he preached, "but he who——without works——believes much in Jesus Christ."

Believing that the Scripture clearly taught man the will of God, Luther pointed out errors in the church's teaching about many things, including relics, prayers to saints and the rule of the pope. In response, Pope Leo called Luther a "child of the devil" and issued a papal bull declaring Luther a heretic, excommunicating him from the church and condemning all his writings. A large crowd of students and professors gathered in the square at Wittenberg University before a great bonfire where Luther read aloud a copy of the papal bull. "This bull condemns me without any proof from Scripture," he said. "If I am a heretic, then show me from God's Word. It is better that I should die a thousand times than I should retract one word of what I have written about the sacred truth of God." Then Luther cast the bull into the flames. Everyone knew that the likely result of Luther's stand against the church would be death by burning. His friends urged him to slow down and keep quiet. But Luther said, "I cannot go against what the Scripture teaches. I am in God's hands."

Martin Luther's message deeply divided Germany. Some rejoiced to learn that salvation came by faith alone in Jesus Christ, while others remained loyal to the teachings of the Roman church. The German Emperor, Charles V, wanted to settle the matter once and for all. In 1521, he called a meeting of the Diet, the council of German princes, at the city of Worms to hear from Luther and representatives of the pope in order to decide Luther's fate.

Before setting out from Wittenberg to Worms, a professor said to him, "Martin, don't go! The emperor hates your ideas. They will burn you alive like they did John Huss."

"I commend my cause to God," Luther answered. "He saved three boys from the fiery furnace, but if He will not save me, my head is worth nothing compared with Christ. This is no time to think about safety."

In Worms, princes, nobles, professors, scholars and church leaders so packed the great hall to standing capacity that only Emperor Charles had room to sit. The eyes of all these powerful and learned men were fixed on Luther, who stood before them dressed in a coarse brown monk's robe.

"Are these your writings," a churchman said, dropping a pile of books and pamphlets on a table in front of Luther.

"The books are all mine, and I have written more," Luther said.

"Do you defend them or will you renounce them and admit your errors?"

Luther looked at the stack of his writings and paused. "This touches God and his Word," he said. "This affects the salvation of souls. Of this Christ said, 'He who denies me before men, him will I deny before my Father.' To say too little or too much would be dangerous. I beg you, give me time to think it over."

The members of the Diet were surprised by Luther's hesitation. After some deliberation, the emperor granted Luther a recess until the following afternoon. The next day, Luther appeared again before the Diet. "Most serene Emperor," Luther said, bowing at the waist, "most illustrious princes, most merciful lords, if I have not given some of you your proper titles, I beg you to forgive me. I am not a courtier, but a monk. I cannot renounce these works unless I am shown from Scripture where I am in error. If I am shown my error from Scripture, I will be the first to throw my books into the fire." Murmurs echoed around the hall and tensions mounted as it became clear that Luther had not come to recant but resist.

His accusers demanded that he accept the decrees of popes and church councils as superior to Scripture itself. "Martin, you claim that you only teach what the Scripture teaches. This is what heretics always say. This is what Wyclif and Huss said. Martin, how can you think that you are the only one to understand Scripture? Are you wiser than the pope and the great church councils? Now answer us simply, do you renounce your books and the errors which they contain?"

"Since your majesty and your lordships desire a simple reply, I will answer," Luther said, sweeping his gaze around the hall. "Unless I am convicted by Scripture and plain reason——I do not accept the authority of popes and councils alone, for they have contradicted each other——my conscience is captive to the Word of God. I cannot and will not recant anything. Here I stand; I cannot do otherwise, so help me God." Supporters of the pope hissed and shouted as Luther left the hall. "Away with him," some cried as they followed him out of the city, howling like wolves. Luther doubted that he would reach Wittenberg alive.

Meanwhile in the great hall, Emperor Charles rose and said, "A single monk cannot be right and the testimony of a thousand years of Christendom be wrong." The princes agreed. They declared Luther an enemy of the state and sentenced him to death. As Luther left Worms and headed into the countryside, a band of armed men on horseback charged out of the woods, seized him and galloped away to an ancient castle perched on the edge of a mountain. However, his kidnappers were not enemies, but friends. Prince Frederick of Saxony, Luther's friend and protector, fearful that Luther might be killed, had arranged the kidnapping. Safe from his enemies, Luther began translating the Bible into German. "I want the people to read the Scriptures for themselves," Luther said. Before long, printing presses cranked out tens of thousands of copies of the German Bible, and the people snatched them up, eager to discover the truths of God's Word.

Luther returned to Wittenberg to preach, teach and write. And how he wrote! Besides his German translation of the Scripture, he wrote commentaries on most of the books of the Bible, scores of books and pamphlets on the Christian faith and a number of hymns. The greatest of these, "A Mighty Fortress Is Our God," became the anthem of the Reformation. He married Katherine von Bora* and raised a family.

At the age of sixty-two, Luther died of a sudden illness. His last prayer was, "Father, into Your hands I commit my spirit, for You have redeemed me." Luther's teachings and writings changed the thinking of a large part of the Christian world. He pointed people to the Scriptures as the only infallible guide for Christian faith and life, and God has used it to change individuals and societies throughout the world.

"Martin Luther: Father of the Reformation" is excerpted from *Trial and Triumph: Stories from Church History* (1999).

---

* Read about Katherine von Bora in Hannula's *Radiant: Fifty Remarkable Women in Church History* (2015).

CHAPTER 6:
HENDRICH VOES
AND JOHANN ESCH

First Martyrs of the Reformation

(c.1485–1523)

In October 1522, soldiers of the Holy Roman Empire battered open the gates of St. Augustine's monastery in Antwerp. They came with orders to arrest the Augustinian monks and shutter the building. Bursting into room after room, they clamped the startled monks in irons, although a few men escaped by climbing over the wall. The soldiers barricaded the entrance to the monastery and marched their captives off to prison.

A year earlier, their prior, James Probst, had been arrested for spreading the teachings of Martin Luther. Luther, an Augustinian monk, taught many Augustinians at Wittenberg University——including James Probst——to study the Scriptures and to follow its teaching above all else. These monks carried Luther's ideas to monas-teries and churches across Western Europe. Since 1519, nearly all the monks at Probst's monastery in Antwerp had followed him in turning away from trying to earn forgiveness with God through their own efforts. They believed that Jesus Christ fully paid for their sins on the cross, and they spread that good news of God's grace in Christ.

However, the pope and Emperor Charles V moved decisively to stamp out the Reformation in the Netherlands.* Antwerp, a rich center of trade and commerce, would not be allowed to separate from the Church of Rome which Charles believed would break the unity of his empire. Evangelical German princes thwarted Charles's efforts to seize Luther and stamp out the spread of Evangelical ideas in Germany. But Charles possessed greater power to enforce his will in the Netherlands.

After church officials threw Prior Probst in prison, they warned the monks of his monastery to stop spreading Luther's teaching. But they kept proclaiming forgiveness in Jesus Christ to the men and women of the city who flocked to hear them preach——jamming the monastery chapel and the nearby church. And so the leaders of church and state decided to crush them.

In prison, the monks faced torture and the threat of being burned alive. Under the intense pressure, they cracked, denied their faith and submitted to the dictates of the Roman church. When they signed a recantation, church authorities assigned them to do penance for their sins and placed them in different monasteries where the priors were commanded to keep a close watch on them. Even their leader, James Probst, broke and recanted. But not long after his release, he repented of his cowardice and openly preached

---

* At that time, the Netherlands referred to the lands comprised by pres-ent-day Belgium and the Netherlands.

forgiveness and eternal life by faith in Christ alone. He was arrested again and sentenced to death. Probst escaped from prison and fled to Germany where he preached the gospel for the rest of his life.

In the meantime, soldiers scoured the towns and villages of the Netherlands in search of the monks who had escaped the raid on the monastery. Eventually, they laid hands on two of them—Hendrich Voes and Johann Esch—cast them into a dungeon cell and threatened them with death if they would not recant. Despite harsh treatment and constant interrogation by inquisitors from the Church of Rome, both men held fast to their faith in Christ. When their captors realized they could not be broken, they made the two monks stand trial in Brussels before a panel of churchmen, including Hochstratten, a chief inquisitor for the Roman church. The accused men testified that the Scriptures alone are the supreme authority for Christians, and that the pope's only duty is to feed the flock from the Word of God.

"Do you believe the decrees of the councils and fathers of the church?" Hochstratten asked.

"When they agree with the Scripture we believe them," they answered.

"Will you retract your belief that the priest does not have the power to pardon sins, and that the power to pardon belongs only to God?" Hochstratten asked.

"No," Voes and Esch replied.

"Do you confess that you have been led astray by Luther?" the inquisitor demanded.

"Just as the apostles were led astray by Jesus Christ," Hendrich Voes said.

Then Hochstratten read out a list of Evangelical teachings, including that sinners are justified only by faith in Christ. "Will you retract these beliefs?" he asked.

"No, we will not retract anything," Esch and Voes answered. "We will not deny the Word of God. We would rather die for the truth of our faith."

The judges conferred with one another for a short time and then said, "Because you refuse to recant——we pronounce you heretics who deserve to be burnt alive. We shall hand you over to the secular power for punishment."

To symbolize that the condemned men were no longer conse- crated priests of the Roman church, clergymen performed a ritual of removing their clerical robes and scraping their hands raw. While the men were being degraded, they prayed, "Thank You, heavenly Father, for delivering us from this false priesthood and making us priests of Your holy order."

Then guards bound them and turned them over to the imperial authorities who readily agreed to burn them for heresy.

On July 1, 1523, soldiers led the monks to the square in the center of Brussels and tied them to a stake. Many of the people who were sympathetic to their cause called out from their windows and rooftops, urging them to be faithful to the end. A large crowd gath- ered around, and many shed tears as they looked at the doomed-to- die young men and marveled at their calm composure and steadfast faith. Observing a wide smile on Voes's face, one churchman said, "Take heed, you are glorifying yourself."

"God forbid that I should glory in anything but the cross of my Lord Jesus Christ," Voes said.

"Put God before your eyes," an inquisitor advised him.

"I trust that I carry Him truly in my heart," Voes replied.

Even at the last minute, Hochstratten and other church officials tried to get them to recant. "We ask you once more," Hochstratten said, "are you willing to receive the Christian faith?"

"We believe in the Christian church," the martyrs answered, "but not in your church."

The authorities instructed the executioner to take his time placing the wood, kindling and straw around the defrocked monks, hoping that they would recant as they contemplated the painful death that awaited them. But the condemned prisoners spent the time singing psalms and occasionally calling out to the crowd, "We are willing to die for the name of Jesus Christ."

"Convert! Convert!" cried the inquisitor, "or you shall die in the name of the devil."

"No," replied Voes and Esch, "we will die like Christians for the truth of the gospel."

When the executioner lit the pile and the fire began to rise around their feet, Hendrich Voes looked at the flames and said, "They seem like roses to me." The men prayed together, saying, "O Lord Jesus, the Son of David, have pity on us!"

Then they recited the Apostles' Creed. As the flames overwhelmed them, they sang praises to God until the breath of life expired. They were the first martyrs of the Protestant Reformation.

In an effort to wipe out the memory of the Evangelical monks of Antwerp, the Augustinian monastery was completely demolished—not one stone was left upon another. A number of citizens of the town who trusted in Christ through the preaching of the monks were thrown in prison. An Evangelical preacher was tied up in a sack and drowned in the river. The authorities banned the Scriptures in the language of the people and burned Evangelical books. "The books leave the shelves, but not the people's hearts," said the humanist scholar, Erasmus.

Luther wept when he heard about the deaths of the two men in Brussels. "Christ is gathering some fruits of our preaching, and preparing new martyrs," he said.

"Praise to the Father of mercies," Luther wrote to the believers in the Netherlands, "for to you it has been given, not only to confess Christ, but to be the first to endure shame, imprisonment and reproach for His name's sake, and now you have proved the strength of your faith by sealing your testimony with your blood. O how shamelessly were these two souls slain, but how gloriously shall they reappear with Christ…Therefore, well beloved, let us be joyful in Christ. Let us pray for one another and reach out a helping hand to each other, and let us cleave with one mind to Christ our Head."

Martin Luther wrote a hymn commemorating the martyrdom of Esch and Voes entitled: "A New Song We Raise." It was widely sung in Germany and the Netherlands. The first verse of its English translation reads,

> Flung to the heedless winds
> Or on the waters cast,
> The martyrs' ashes, watched,
> Shall gathered be at last.
> And from that scattered dust,
> Around us and abroad,
> Shall spring a plenteous seed
> Of witnesses for God.

Many witnesses for God did spring up in Brussels and Antwerp and beyond. "Two are burnt in Brussels," one Roman Catholic citizen complained, "and the whole city begins to favor Luther. In every place where they raise a stake for burning, they sow a field of heretics."

Although fierce persecution against Protestants raged for decades, the good news of Christ——for which Voes and Esch died——reaped a great harvest of souls across the Netherlands.

CHAPTER 7:
PHILIP MELANCHTHON

Nothing Except Heaven
(1497–1560)

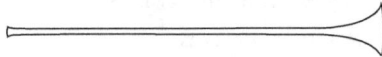

In 1530, things looked bad for the Evangelicals of Germany. Emperor Charles V of the Holy Roman Empire wanted to crush them and their leader, Martin Luther. When the Protestant states of Germany met to form a mutual defense pact against the emperor, they argued and failed to act. The emperor, hoping to dominate the German Protestants without having to go to war, called for a conference of Roman Catholic and Evangelical church leaders in Augsburg "to consult and decide about the disturbances and dissensions in the holy faith and Christian religion."

At first, Prince John, the Elector of Saxony, planned to have Martin Luther head the delegation of Evangelical theologians. But Luther stood condemned by the pope and banned as an outlaw by the emperor. So the elector assigned Philip Melanchthon——a professor of Greek and theology at the University of Wittenberg and Luther's closest friend——to be the chief spokesman for the Protestant cause. He didn't want the job. Melanchthon was a renowned classical scholar, not a controversialist. "Why have I, born for my Greek studies and for the humble pursuits of the scholar, been set in the high places of theological debates and war? If only Doctor Martin had been with us, he would have saved it all!"

It fell to Melanchthon to write a defense of Evangelical teaching. He strove to present the basic truths of Christianity as simply as possible. For two months, Melanchthon endured sleepless nights as he labored over every word of the statement of the Evangelical faith. He wrote and rewrote and constantly sought the advice of other theologians, especially Luther with whom he exchanged letters frequently. Melanchthon's mastery of the Greek and Latin classics and philosophy honed his skill to express ideas concisely, clearly and beautifully.

When Luther read a draft, he said, "I know not how to improve it." Luther appreciated his godly character and remarkable talents. "I was born," Luther said, "only for the field of battle and to fight with demons. Hence my writings are full of war and tempest. But Philip advances slowly and gently——he sows and waters joyfully——according to the gifts which God has bestowed on him with such a liberal hand."

When Melanchthon completed the *Augsburg Confession,* as his statement of faith was called, the elector of Saxony and the leaders of all the Protestant cities and provinces of Germany signed it. On June 25, 1530, the conference gathered in the chapel of the bishop of Augsburg's palace to hear the Evangelicals defend their faith. Emperor Charles sat on his throne, surrounded by crimson-robed princes, dignitaries and a crowd of bishops and archbishops wearing their episcopal miters. Melanchthon's confession of faith was read out in German, impressing all open-minded listeners with its clarity, simplicity and firm grounding in the Scriptures. The theologians from the Church of Rome insisted that good works were necessary for justification. "We cannot be justified before God by our own strength, merit, or works," Melanchthon wrote, "but we are justified on account of Christ——by grace through faith. His death made satisfaction for our sins. This faith is the righteousness which God imputes to the sinner."

"You must submit to the pope and the councils of the church," the Roman Catholic authorities said.

"It is not necessary to obey the bishops," the confession stated, "if they teach anything contrary to the Scriptures of God. We accept no doctrine or ceremony contrary to the holy Scripture."

A Roman Catholic duke from Bavaria, after listening to Melanchthon speak, said to John Eck, the chief spokesman for the Catholic theologians, "You assured us that the Lutherans could easily be refuted. Can you answer that?"

"I can refute it from the writings of the church fathers," Eck said, "but not from the Scriptures."

"Then," the duke replied, "the Lutherans stand in the Scriptures, and we Catholics stand outside of them."

The conference continued for several weeks, and the Roman Catholic theologians kept demanding that the Evangelicals submit to the absolute authority of the pope and church councils. Cardinal Campeggio went further, urging the emperor to wage war on the Evangelicals. "Extirpate the poisonous plant by fire and sword," he advised Emperor Charles.

Charles decreed that the Protestants must abandon any beliefs and practices not approved by the Church of Rome. Later, he threatened to use force if they failed to comply within six months. On the conference floor, Cardinal Campeggio demanded that the

Protestants yield to the teachings of the Roman church. Then Melanchthon stood up and looked at all the assembled dignitaries. "We cannot yield, nor desert the truth," he said. "We pray——that for God's sake in Christ——our opponents will grant us that which we cannot surrender with a good conscience."

"I cannot, I cannot," Campeggio shouted! "The keys of papal authority do not err."

"We will commit our cause to God," Melanchthon said. "If God be for us, who can be against us? We will toil and fight and die, if God so wills, rather than betray the souls in our care."

"You would think him a mere lad," one man said of Melanchthon, "but in intellect, learning and talent, he is a giant. One cannot conceive how such heights of genius and wisdom can be enclosed in such a little body."

Although fierce trials lay in store, the *Augsburg Confession* firmly planted Evangelical doctrine in the world never to be uprooted.

Roman Catholic theologians fiercely criticized Melanchthon's writings and savagely attacked his character. "He is a minister of Satan," one wrote. The controversy wounded his gentle spirit. "What utterly lays me low is strife and controversy," Melanchthon confided to a friend. "God is my witness that my intentions have been good. My reward is that I shall be hated."

Melanchthon longed to return to the calm life of a university professor, but that was not to be. Time and again, Protestant rulers called on him to expound and defend the gospel at conferences throughout Germany. "What tempests are these that drive me," he wrote a friend, "from the quiet and more useful studies I love into the heart of these bitter controversies which I abhor?"

He did it all without neglecting his university duties. Melanchthon lectured several times a day, beginning at 7 o'clock in the morning. He slept from 9:00 p.m. until 2:00 a.m. when he arose, lit his oil lamp and resumed his studies. Luther worried about Melanchthon's health. Once when they were eating dinner together, Melanchthon scribbled notes for a book as he ate. Luther grabbed the pen out of his hand and said, "Dear Philip, we can serve God not only by work, but also by rest."

Students flocked to hear Melanchthon's Greek lectures on Homer and the Apostle Paul. He wrote *Commonplaces*, the first Protestant systematic theology. "In this most beautiful book——a book of gold," Luther told his students, "you will find pure theology stated in a quiet and orderly way."

Melanchthon published commentaries on several books of the Bible, two books on rhetoric, a treatise on the Lord's Supper and several translations of Greek and Latin classics. He wrote hundreds of letters each year to monarchs, theologians, magistrates and friends across Europe. The heavy workload took its toll. "For the last three years," he told a colleague, "I feel as if I must sink and die."

Then, in 1540, while visiting the city of Weimar, Melanchthon collapsed. He grew delirious, didn't recognize his friends and stopped eating. Luther rushed to Melanchthon's side and found him nearly comatose. Seeing him on the verge of death, Luther wept and prayed fervently for his life. Then, taking Melanchthon's hand, Luther said, "Be of good cheer, my friend Philip, you will not die. Trust in the Lord who can wound and bind up, can smite and heal again."

A few hours later, Melanchthon breathed deeply, weakly raised his head and whispered to Luther, "I am now on a good journey. I beg you, let me go."

"We can't spare you yet, Philip," Luther told him. "You must serve our God a little longer."

Luther spoon fed his friend, cajoled him to press on and prayed for his recovery. "If Luther had not come to me," Melanchthon said after regaining his strength, "I should certainly have died."

The year 1546 cast dark clouds of trouble over Melanchthon. Emperor Charles V made peace with France, his adversary to the west, and with the Turks, his great enemy to the east. This freed him to concentrate his forces on crushing the German Protestants. As the emperor prepared for war, Martin Luther died. "The charioteer of Israel is gone," the grieving Melanchthon told the students at Wittenberg University.

Many years earlier, Melanchthon had said of Luther, "I embrace him with all my heart. I would rather die than be separated from him." They had made an effective team. Melanchthon's tact and gentleness helped to balance Luther's blunt and bold personality. And now, when the Evangelicals of Germany faced their greatest peril, Luther was gone.

The emperor's armies crushed the Protestant forces that tried to stop them. Imperial soldiers took the elector of Saxony prisoner and laid siege to Wittenberg. The professors closed Wittenberg University, and the students and faculty fled the city. Melanchthon took comfort in the fact that Christ would not forsake His flock. "Lo! I am with you always even to the end of the world," Melanchthon said. "He will preserve the people that maintain the doctrines of the gospel and truly call upon His name."

Although defeated temporarily, the Protestant princes soon rose up, made a secret treaty with France and defeated the imperial forces in battle. And Charles grudgingly granted Protestantism official status within the Holy Roman Empire. The faith that Luther and Melanchthon had struggled for was secured.

In 1560, as Melanchthon lay on his deathbed, a relative asked him, "Do you want anything?" Melanchthon replied, "Nothing except heaven."

REFORMATION BASICS 2

Sola Gratia and Sola Fide
("By Grace Alone" and "Through Faith Alone")

Paul wrote in Ephesians 2:8-9: "For by grace you have been saved through faith. And this is not your own doing; it is the gift of God, not a result of works, so that no one may boast."

Although the Scriptures clearly teach that peace with God and eternal life are gifts of God's free grace received by faith in Christ alone, the medieval church rejected this doctrine. It taught that salvation came in stages by believing in Christ, receiving God's grace through the sacraments of the church and doing good works, and condemned anyone who taught otherwise.

Martin Luther's life was transformed when he understood the Bible's message of justification by faith in Christ. "I saw that God had given me the righteousness of Christ through faith," Luther said. "Christ suffered all the penalty for my sin on the cross. By faith Christ's righteousness becomes my righteousness."

Luther and the other reformers embraced this biblical truth and it became the foundation of their preaching and writing. Perhaps the most beautiful expression of *sola fide* and *sola gratia* (justification by grace alone, through faith alone) is found in question 60 of the Heidelberg Catechism.

Question: How are you right with God?

Answer: Only by true faith in Jesus Christ. Even though my conscience accuses me of having grievously sinned against all God's commandments and of never having kept any of them, and even though I am still inclined toward all evil, nevertheless, without my deserving it at all, out of sheer grace, God grants and credits to me the perfect satisfaction, righteousness, and holiness of Christ, as if I had never sinned nor been a sinner, as if I had been as perfectly obedient as Christ was obedient for me. All I need to do is to accept this gift of God with a believing heart.

CHAPTER 8:
MARTIN BUCER

Champion of Protestant Unity
(1491–1551)

———————⊲

One afternoon in April 1518, university students, profes-sors, courtiers, burghers, priests and friars packed the great hall of the Augustinian monastery in Heidelberg, Germa-ny, to hear Martin Luther. Six months earlier, Luther had nailed Ninety-five Theses against indulgences on a church door in Witten-berg. Since then, his writings had spawned debate about Christian doctrine across Europe. In the audience sat Martin Bucer, a black-robed Dominican friar with his tonsured head bent over pen and paper, scribbling notes furiously as Luther spoke. His heart leapt for joy when Luther said, "Man is not justified before God because of his many works. He is justified apart from his works through faith in Christ."

When Luther finished laying out his points, theologians peppered him with questions and accused him of teaching against church tradition. "Luther solved all objections," Bucer told a friend. "His concise answers drawn from the Word of God astonished everyone."

After Luther's presentation, Bucer rushed forward to talk with him. Luther invited Bucer to supper. For several hours, they ate and talked. Luther explained his understanding of Paul's letter to the Romans. "The Christian," he said, "is a sinner and righteous at the same time. In Christ he is righteous and perfect—in himself he is unrighteous and sinful." With a broad smile, Luther insisted that Christians can be full of hope, striving to serve God, not for who they are, but for who Christ is. Bucer left a changed man, trusting in Christ's sacrifice on the cross and believing that his faith was a gift of God's grace.

When Bucer returned to his monastery, he used his knowledge of Greek to carefully search the Scriptures for himself. The more he studied the Word of God, the more he saw how far the church had drifted from the Bible's Christ-centered message. When he began to teach his fellow monks justification by faith in Christ alone, he encountered fierce resistance. Once, his comments so enraged the monks that they came close to stoning him on the spot. Not long after, Bucer left the monastery for good.

A few years later, he got married and became the pastor of a church in Weissembourg, Germany. His congregation never had a priest like him before. He preached every day of the week and twice on Sunday, making his way through whole books of the Bible. For the first time, his flock heard about God's love and not only His judgment. "Trust God freely," he told them, "and find comfort in Him as in a father, since He cares for us and loves us more than a father his son or a mother her helpless infant."

Many trusted in Christ alone for the complete forgiveness of their sins and started to live for Him. But Bucer's ministry got him excommunicated by the bishop and expelled from Weissembourg. Without money or work, he fled with his wife to Strasbourg, a city of the Holy Roman Empire that had embraced the Reformation through the preaching of Matthew Zell. Zell invited Bucer to teach in his home while city officials rebuffed demands from the Roman church and the imperial government to banish Bucer from Strasbourg.

Bucer's persuasive and biblical teaching won a growing number of hearers. Before long, he became a pastor of a parish church. "Look to Christ only," Bucer preached. "Forgiveness of sins can only be found in Him." While pointing his congregation to Jesus, he called them to obey His commandment to love one another. "Let us rejoice with all our hearts that it is our duty to serve our fellow man and show him the greatest compassion," Bucer said, "for in so doing we display a modest share of gratitude to our most merciful Father and Savior."

Carefully explaining the Scriptures, verse by verse, he preached through the New Testament and through many Old Testament books. He labored to set the historical context to give the meaning that the biblical authors intended. "It is necessary that nothing other than the certain words of God be preached," he said.

Bucer, with the other Evangelical ministers, began to reorganize church worship according to the Scriptures. They replaced the Latin mass with a worship service in German that included a substantial sermon from the Bible and congregational psalm singing. Like a nurturing shepherd, Bucer visited the sick and the poor and went house to house encouraging parents and teaching their children. He divided the parish into small groups and assigned spiritually-mature men to oversee the church families in their neighborhoods.

The reformers of Strasbourg created an educational system for the city's youth. Unusual for the time, they established schools for girls as well as boys. "The hope of all rests upon you." Bucer told the students. They converted a former monastery into a boarding school to teach and equip young men for the ministry. Students from all over Germany and Switzerland came to Strasbourg to study the Scriptures and learn to pastor.

Clergy and laymen throughout Europe read Bucer's published commentaries on the gospels, Paul's letters and several Old Testament prophets. A number of cities that considered joining the Reformation invited Bucer to present Evangelical teaching and debate with Roman Catholic theologians. His knowledge of Scripture and his winsome manner won many to the Reformed faith. "I wish that you could have seen and heard what grace God bestowed on Bucer as he responded to all the objections of his opponents," one reformer said.

Meanwhile, persecution against Protestants raged across Europe. "Poor and simple Christians——men, women and children——are being slaughtered," one observer recorded. "They abandon their countries and leave behind all their possessions." Many of these benighted people found refuge in Strasbourg. "The persecuted come here," one Strasbourg pastor said, "and from here they are sent out again to serve the Word of God."

Bucer always opened his house to refugees fleeing persecution——even after a plague swept through Strasbourg, killing hundreds of his parishioners, including his wife Elizabeth and three of their children. One of those who found shelter in his home was the Italian reformer, Peter Martyr Vermigli. "I have never seen Bucer inactive," Vermigli said. "He spends his time either preaching or looking after the church. After working all day, he devotes his nights to study and prayer. Seldom did I wake up and not find him awake as well."

In 1538, John Calvin, the exiled French reformer, came to Strasbourg. Bucer welcomed him into his home and encouraged Calvin to become the pastor of French refugees in the city. Bucer became a mentor and father figure to Calvin. "Martin Bucer is unsurpassed by anyone today," Calvin said, "for his profound scholarship, his great knowledge, his keen mind, his wide reading, and many other virtues."

These were difficult and dangerous times for the Evangelicals of Europe. Charles V, the Emperor of the Holy Roman Empire——determined to keep his far-flung territories united in the Church of Rome——burned the books of Luther, Bucer and other reformers and threatened to stamp out the Evangelical faith. Protestant rulers like Philip of Hesse and John Frederick of Saxony wanted the Evangelical provinces and free cities of the empire to unite for mutual protection against the emperor.

However, at the time that Protestant unity was most critical, a dispute over the precise meaning of the Lord's Supper bitterly divided them. In books and pamphlets, they promoted their understanding of the Supper and harshly criticized the views of the other reformers. The enemies of the Reformation declared that the disagreements among the Protestants proved that the only true church was the Church of Rome. Bucer labored with might and main to bring the Protestants together for the honor of Christ and the winning of souls. "My dear brothers," Bucer wrote, "it is enough if we agree on the fundamentals of the faith——that we are all nothing and that God wants to save us and make us holy through Christ alone."

At the Marburg Colloquy in 1529, the principal reformers gathered to discuss their differences. (A colloquy is a meeting talk over theological issues.) Bucer cajoled the reformers to unite as brothers and find common ground. Even though they agreed on every doctrine except some of the particulars of the Lord's presence in the Supper, Luther said that he did not consider Bucer and the Swiss reformers fellow brothers in Christ.

"If you immediately condemn anyone who doesn't quite believe the same as you do," Bucer said later, "who, pray tell, can you still consider a brother?"

Although dejected, Bucer did not give up striving for Protestant unity in the Lord's Supper. Bucer emphasized that the Supper was more than just a memorial, and that Christ was truly present——but spiritually present. "That is why we are reminded of the death of Christ," Bucer wrote about the sacrament, "in order that we may believe that we are saved by His death. Wherever this happens, Christ is truly in our midst, and our souls are fed——not with the bread and wine——but with the Lord Jesus Christ Himself."

His efforts to unite the Evangelical camps often met with derision. Many of the Swiss reformers accused Bucer of compromising Scripture truth in order to satisfy the Lutherans. Both sides lashed out with harsh language, calling him "a knave, a fanatic and a servant of the devil." But Bucer refused to let personal attacks and cutting criticism keep him from loving his brothers and treating them with respect. "We must seek unity and love in our relationships with everyone," Bucer wrote a friend, "regardless of how they behave towards us."

For nearly thirty years, Bucer worked tirelessly to bring the European reformers together. "We should attempt as much as possible to use every means to unite all God-fearing people in Christ, our

Lord," he said. To achieve his goal, Bucer wrote thousands of letters and traveled thousands of miles on horseback over the muddy and dangerous roads of the empire. "I certainly believe that we could come to an agreement on those things that are truly fundamental to the Christian faith," Bucer said, "and leave the rest to Christian freedom——if we would only focus on God with all our hearts."

By 1549, the armies of Emperor Charles V had defeated the Protestant forces of Germany. He threatened the German cities with destruction if they failed to abandon the Reformation and return to the Church of Rome. When the city leaders of Strasbourg complied with the emperor's demands, they removed Bucer from his post. Turning down offers of sanctuary from Melanchthon in Wittenberg and Calvin in Geneva, he accepted an invitation from Thomas Cranmer, the archbishop of Canterbury, to come to England. Edward VI personally welcomed Bucer to his kingdom and appointed him professor of theology at Cambridge University. Bucer taught young men preparing for the ministry and worked with Cranmer in revising the *Book of Common Prayer*. "It is our business to restore the simplicity of Christ and the apostles and the early church," he advised the English, "and introduce nothing that is not found in the Word of God."

But Bucer struggled with recurring sicknesses in England, and in 1551 he died. University officials buried him with honors in Great St. Mary's Church in Cambridge. When word reached John Calvin in Geneva, he said, "I feel like my heart is going to break when I think of the great loss the church of God has sustained in the death of Bucer."

A few years later, when the Roman Catholic Queen Mary ascended the throne in London, she outlawed the Evangelical faith, imprisoning and executing Protestants. In 1556, she had the bones of Martin Bucer dug up and burned in the market square of Cambridge. But that did not end the influence of the great champion of Protestant unity. His views on worship, Christian community, the training of pastors and the spiritual presence of Christ in the Lord's Supper shaped many ministers, including John Calvin, who put them into practice in Geneva and further developed them in his writings. And through those who followed Calvin, they spread to the whole world.

CHAPTER 9:
KATHERINE ZELL

The Mother of the Reformers
(1497–1562)

In July 1524, an Evangelical pastor and 150 men of his congregation arrived in Strasbourg, Germany, with little more than the clothes on their backs. A few days before, they had been driven from Kenzingen, their home town, by order of the imperial government because of their faith. As the weary and downcast men stood in the city square and told their story to curious Strasbourgers, Katherine Zell arrived on the scene and took charge. "Welcome, my dear brothers in the Lord," the twenty-six-year-old woman told the men. "Please follow me."

She led the men to the large parsonage where Katherine lived with her husband, Matthew Zell, a popular preacher and the first man to proclaim the Reformation in Strasbourg. She flung open the doors of her home and housed eighty of them under her own roof. With borrowed blankets, Katherine created makeshift beds that filled the hallways and the floors of every room. Pleading door-to-door, she persuaded her neighbors to take in a few of the outcasts. Before nightfall, all the men were lodged. Little did Katherine know that she would spend the rest of her life caring for refugees.

Katherine sent an open letter to the exiles' wives left in Kenzingen. "To my fellow sisters in Christ," she wrote, "day and night I pray that God may increase your faith and that you will not forget His invincible Word. Remember the Word of the Lord in Isaiah 54:8, 'In overflowing anger for a moment I hid My face from you, but with everlasting love I will have compassion on you.'"

Just a few months before, the Reverend Martin Bucer had presided over the wedding ceremony of Katherine and Matthew Zell. In 1519, after reading the writings of Martin Luther, Matthew Zell began to preach justification by faith alone. Many in his congregation rejoiced at the good news that through faith in Christ, God declares them righteous in His sight. Excited crowds filled the cathedral to hear him. But the bishop of Strasbourg charged him with heresy, declaring that no Evangelical doctrines should be preached until they were approved by a general council of the church. "We are told," Zell wrote to the leaders of church and state, "to make no innovations but to wait for the decisions of a general council. If the apostles had waited for a general council of the Jews to endorse Christ, they would have waited a very long time. Scripture, my lords, send out preachers of the Scripture. If you do not, they will come anyway. And though you issue a thousand bulls against them, though you use up the whole Black Forest to burn them, though you scatter them over the earth, it will do you no good. If you root them out, from their roots others will grow."

The bishop tried to ban Zell from all the churches of the city, but Zell's popularity among the people and the city council prevented the bishop from silencing him. The council insisted that Strasbourg Cathedral hold both Roman Catholic and Evangelical services. The bishop's men performed mass at the high altar before dwindling numbers of worshipers. Matthew Zell preached to several thousand in the nave from a portable wooden pulpit that his friends wheeled in and out of the cathedral. "Why do they persecute the teachers of the truth?" Zell said. "I will tell you—because they know indulgences and purgatory are false, and they will get no more money."

Early in 1523, Martin Bucer arrived in Strasbourg with his wife shortly after being banished from his preaching post and excommunicated from the Church of Rome. He was one of the first Protestant ministers to get married. For centuries the Church of Rome did not permit priests to marry. Matthew Zell took the Bucers into his home. The Bucers' lovely example of Christian marriage inspired Matthew and other ministers to consider marriage.

Soon, Zell fell in love with Katherine Schutz, the well-educated daughter of a Strasbourg carpenter. Although Katherine had been a pious girl from her earliest days, she lacked the assurance that God forgave her sins in Christ, believing that she needed to do more to win God's favor. "I had a great struggle," she said. "In all my works of service to God I found no certainty of the love and grace of God. I felt sick, near to death. I was like the poor diseased woman in the gospel who spent all her money on physicians, but when she heard of Christ, she came to Him and was helped by Him. So it was with me and many others with stricken hearts. But God had mercy on us. He raised up the worthy Doctor Martin Luther and sent him out to speak and write."

Katherine wrote to Luther and revealed her spiritual turmoil. He wrote back, encouraging her to put all her trust in Christ. "So beautifully did he write to me of the Lord Jesus Christ," Katherine said later, "that it was as if I was drawn out of the pit—out of grim, bitter hell itself into the blessed sweet kingdom of heaven."

Luther's message of justification by faith alone drew her to Christ, and she wanted to dedicate her life to lead others to the Savior. When Matthew Zell proposed marriage, Katherine happily accepted because she admired him as a kind and faithful man of God. He appreciated her bright mind and strong character, and he viewed her as his partner in ministry. As one of the first Evangelical pastor's wives, Katherine knew that she would be closely observed. "I myself married a priest with the intention of encouraging and making a way for all Christians," she said.

Not long after their wedding, the Church of Rome excommunicated Matthew and called for his arrest and trial as a heretic. The Strasbourg city council ignored the demand. Roman churchmen spread ugly rumors about the Zells. They claimed that they argued constantly and often came to blows. Katherine wrote in their defense. "My husband and I have never had an unpleasant fifteen minutes," she declared. "We are of one mind and one soul. Christ is the goal before our eyes."

Strasbourg, a "free city" of the Holy Roman Empire, enjoyed a measure of freedom from the control of Emperor Charles V. This enabled Evangelical preachers, with the cooperation of the city council, to proclaim the Scriptures without fear of arrest and execution. It also made Strasbourg a city of refuge for the persecuted.

Not long after the exiles from Kenzingen arrived, the outbreak of the Peasants' War led thousands of displaced women and children to stream into Strasbourg, straining the city's resources. Civic leaders housed most of the refugees in a large church. Katherine labored night and day organizing the distribution of food and urging Strasbourg families to open their hearts and their homes to the refugees. Before the year was out, the war subsided, and the exiles left Strasbourg and went back to their farms. But scarcely a month passed before new groups of people sought haven in Strasbourg.

The Zells always gave consolation, meals and a warm bed to weary travelers or benighted refugees. In 1529, the Swiss reformers, Zwingli and Oecolampadius, came to Strasbourg on their way to the Marburg conference. They stayed for two weeks with the Zells, preparing with Matthew and Martin Bucer their arguments for the great Evangelical meeting on the Lord's Supper with Luther and Melanchthon. "For fourteen days I was cook and maid while the dear men, Oecolampadius and Zwingli, were here," Katherine said.

The reformers were impressed by Katherine's lively faith and her deep knowledge of the Scriptures. "She knows and searches the mysteries of Christ," Martin Bucer said.

Katherine's heart broke when word came from the Marburg conference that Luther was unwilling to reach an agreement on the Lord's Supper with the Swiss reformers, and that he had even refused to shake their hands as fellow Christians. Katherine wrote Luther and challenged him to show love and patience to his brothers in Christ with whom he disagreed.

When the reformer John Calvin fled France and arrived in Strasbourg penniless, Katherine and Matthew took him in for a time. A few years later, they welcomed him back when he was expelled from Geneva. Through the years, Katherine hosted many of the most influential reformers of Europe.

Katherine and Matthew rejoiced at the births of their two children, but joy soon turned to mourning as both of the children died in infancy. At times, Katherine wrestled with bouts of depression. In those dark times, she drew near to Christ for comfort and strength. "Lord Christ," she prayed, "make me live in You." The comfort she received from Him, she freely gave to others. Katherine filled her days visiting and caring for the sick and needy. She knew that her heavenly Father used suffering to sanctify His children. "Bear the cross of the Lord," Katherine often told those enduring hardships.

"Her zeal is incredible for Christ's lowly and afflicted," Martin Bucer said of Katherine. "She is a saintly woman and as God-fearing and courageous as a hero."

In addition to ministering to the downtrodden, Katherine wrote religious tracts, taught women's Bible studies, advised the council on the refugees' needs and spearheaded the effort to make Christian literature available to the poor. Katherine oversaw the publication of a little book of German hymns that sold for a few pennies. "I think it is excellent that folks sing with hearty zeal and clear voice the songs of their salvation," Katherine wrote in the preface. "God is glad when the craftsman at his bench, the maid at the sink, the farmer at the plow, the dresser at the vines and the mother at the cradle break forth in hymns of prayer, praise and instruction."

Some people complained that a woman should not play such a prominent role in the church and accused Katherine of acting as if she were a minister and theologian. They mockingly referred to her as "Doctor Katherine." But Matthew supported her wholeheartedly. "My husband was willing to suffer the want of me at home at times," she said, "that I might better serve the church, and he loved me the more for it. I am not usurping the office of preacher or apostle. I am like the dear Mary Magdalene, who with no thought of being an apostle, came to tell the disciples that she had encountered the risen Lord."

At that time, Anabaptists faced fierce persecution from Roman Catholics and Protestants alike. Many reformers denounced them harshly and wanted them driven out of Protestant cities and lands. Katherine Zell and her husband, although they disagreed with some of their beliefs, saw them as brothers and sisters in Christ. When a group of Strasbourg ministers asked Matthew to call for the expulsion of Anabaptists, he told them, "Leave the Baptists alone and preach Christ."

"Anyone that acknowledges the Lord Christ," Matthew said, "to be the true Son of God and the only Savior of men, will share our table."

"We must share with them in heaven," Katherine added, "whether they are followers of our dear Doctor Luther or Zwingli or the Baptists. We are not bound to be of every opinion and creed, we are bound to show everyone love and service and mercy, for so Christ has taught us. These poor Baptists confess Christ the Lord and His redemption through free grace as we do. If in other things they differ, must we therefore persecute them and Christ in them? The good Samaritan, when he came upon the man who had fallen among thieves, did not ask him to what denomination he belonged, but put him on his donkey and took him to an inn."

Matthew Zell died in January 1548. Katherine lived another fifteen years, serving others with all her strength. For the hospitality and encouragement she offered the leading ministers of the German, Swiss and French Reformations and for the correspondence she maintained with several of them, Katherine became known as the "Mother of the Reformers." But she simply called herself, "a piece of the rib of the blessed Matthew Zell."

CHAPTER 10:
OLAF PETRI

Foremost Reformer of Sweden

(1493–1552)

In 1520, King Christian of Denmark invaded Sweden and took the Swedish crown by force. In what appeared to be an effort to unite the country, he declared a general amnesty and invited the leading bishops and nobles to his coronation in Stockholm—whether they had supported his claim to the throne or had fought for Swedish independence. But King Christian and his ally, Archbishop Trolle, the leading churchman in Sweden, used the occasion to destroy their enemies. On the third day of the coronation festivities, Danish soldiers rounded up two bishops and eighty influential citizens and brought them bound to the marketplace in the city center. Olaf Petri, a Swedish minister and close assistant of Bishop Gregersson of Strängnäs, ran to the marketplace. Through the armed guards who cordoned off the square, he saw the head of Bishop Gregersson laying at the feet of an axman. "Oh!" Petri cried out. "What a tyrannical and unmanly deed to kill a pious bishop!"

Immediately, soldiers grabbed Olaf Petri and pulled him into the square, intending to execute him with the rest. Just then, a German who was visiting Stockholm who had known Petri when they were students at Wittenberg University in Germany, shouted, "Spare him! He is not a Swede, but German! Spare him for God's sake!" Incredibly, the soldiers took the man's word for it and released Petri. They executed the remaining prisoners and burned their bodies.

Shaken to the core, Petri returned to Strängnäs without his beloved bishop, yet convinced that God had spared his life so that he could preach the good news of Jesus Christ.

Four years earlier, Olaf Petri left Sweden to study in Wittenberg. He saw Luther's Ninety-five Theses nailed to the church door in Wittenberg and witnessed the firestorm that it ignited in Europe. Not long after he arrived, Martin Luther began to give his famous university lectures on the epistle to the Romans. For most of his life, Luther had sought forgiveness and peace with God by performing every duty recommended by the church, but his sin and guilt remained. Then when studying Romans, a verse leapt out at him. "For in the gospel a righteousness from God is revealed, a righteousness that is by faith from first to last, just as it is written: 'The righteous will live by faith.'" (Rom. 1:17)

The truth of God revealed in that verse transformed Luther's life. "I felt that I was reborn and had gone through open doors to paradise," he said. "Christ suffered the entire penalty for my sin on the cross. By faith, Christ's righteousness becomes my righteousness."

Full of joy and confidence, Luther taught his students that sinners who trust in Christ no longer have God as their judge but their

Father. Petri followed Luther in putting all his faith and hope in Jesus Christ. "My whole life must be a constant offering of praise and thanks to God for His benefits, grace, and mercy," Petri said. "Praise and glory be to Him forever."

After Olaf Petri completed his degree, he returned to Sweden, anxious to preach true faith in Christ to his countrymen. Soon, Bishop Gregersson who favored the Reformation called him to preach in Strängnäs Cathedral and teach at the cathedral seminary. For his sermons, Petri followed Luther's pattern, beginning with a clear and simple explanation of the text and then applying the message to the hearts of his hearers. "God is angry with the sins of men," he preached. "But in His infinite mercy, God sent Jesus Christ into this world to be a mediator between God and those who have offended Him. Christ's suffering and death made satisfaction for sins and turned away God's wrath for all those who follow Christ and put their trust in Him."

He made it clear that salvation was a gift of God's grace and not earned in any way by good works. "Receive the precious treasure of Christ by faith," Petri said. "Paul took such pains to make it clear to everyone that righteousness comes not from works but from faith in Jesus Christ to all that believe. We receive; we do not give."

Petri taught the Bible as the supreme authority for believers, far above the traditions and teachings of the Church of Rome. "The Word of God is found in holy Scripture which comprises all that man needs to know in order to be saved," he preached. "There is no other sure foundation than the Word of God."

Olaf Petri denounced the lazy priests who failed to feed the flock from the Word of God. "The Holy Spirit has made you overseers to the church of the Lord that He purchased with His own blood," he told them. "You are commanded by God to preach the Word of

God; this is the chief duty of your office. Therefore, he who neglects to preach neglects his entire office."

Many priests and monks bitterly opposed his preaching and stirred up the people against him. "We will not hear this Lutheran heretic!" they shouted. They carried stones into church and pelted him with them as he preached. Often, he finished a sermon bloodied and bruised. Several times, he barely escaped with his life. But he pressed on. Petri's fearless preaching and his lectures on the New Testament in the seminary won many to Christ, including his brother Lars and a deacon of the cathedral named Lars Anderson. These two men together with Olaf became the chief reformers of the Swedish church. From Strängnäs, young preachers spread the gospel to every town and village in the kingdom.

After Bishop Gregersson and the others were killed in the Stockholm Massacre, supporters of Swedish independence rebelled against the Danish king. Under the leadership of Gustavus Vasa, an heir to the Swedish throne, they drove the Danes from Sweden, and the hated Archbishop Trolle fled with them. By the summer of 1523, the Estates of Nobles chose Gustavus king of Sweden. Wanting to learn about the Evangelical faith, Gustavus heard sermons from Olaf Petri and Lars Anderson. Soon the king became a supporter of the Reformation. When Petri preached at Gustavus's coronation, he told the audience that God called them to give obedience to the king, but he also challenged Gustavus to rule justly as a Christian monarch. "Your majesty was not set on the throne to rule over subjects," Olaf preached, "but over your own brothers and sisters who are God's people."

In 1525, opposition to Olaf Petri increased when he got married. Roman Catholic law forbade ministers to marry. A prominent bishop demanded that King Gustavus banish Petri from the kingdom.

"Stop this infection," the bishop told the king, "stop this Lutheran heresy, this heresy of Lucifer."

Petri showed the king from the Scriptures that God did not prohibit marriage for ministers. The king sided with Petri. Gustavus used his royal power to protect the Evangelical preachers and supported their efforts to reform the church.

In an effort to spread the Evangelical message, the king called for a public debate between the reformers and the supporters of the Church of Rome. The Catholic proponent spoke Latin and argued from church tradition and the pronouncements of popes and church councils. Petri spoke Swedish and defended Evangelical teaching solely from the Scriptures. When asked if Christians should pray to saints, Petri answered, "Do not put your trust in any human being, such as the Virgin Mary or any other saint, but trust in God alone."

Most of the audience agreed that Petri won the debate.

Olaf Petri poured all his energies into proclaiming the Word of God. He preached, debated, lectured and wrote. Noblemen and peasants throughout the kingdom read his books on Christian teaching and his printed sermons. He wrote a worship manual for services in the Swedish language and edited the first song book for worship in Swedish that included four hymns that he penned himself. He later expanded the song book, and it formed the basis of Swedish sung praise for generations.

Petri's translation of the New Testament into Swedish in 1526 was his greatest achievement. In most lands, Roman church law only permitted the Scriptures in Latin, and only the well-educated knew Latin. Petri wanted the people to be able to read and understand God's Word for themselves. He strove to bring to life the powerful words as they were first written by the apostles. With royal approval, the Swedish New Testament rolled off the presses and was eagerly read in manors, cloisters and cottages across the land. With the help of his brother Lars, Petri completed the translation of the Old Testament in Swedish in 1541.

When the pope ordered Gustavus to reinstate Archbishop Trolle who had worked with the Danish king to massacre Bishop Gregersson and the nobles in Stockholm, Gustavus informed the pope that Sweden would never again submit to the "heavy yoke of foreign oppressors."

Gustavus forbade any payments to go to the pope. Then the king cast his eyes on the vast lands in Sweden controlled by the Church of Rome. He seized one monastery, turned out the monks and made it his own estate. To win the support of noblemen, Gustavus pledged to return to them any land that their ancestors had donated to the church under the belief that it would shorten their time of punishment in purgatory. The reformers demonstrated from the Scriptures that there was no such place as purgatory. "When we become one with Christ," Petri preached, "we surely shall remain with Him in eternity." He argued that God the Father would not punish believers in Christ after death since He already punished their sins through Christ's death on the cross. "Now God no longer sees them as sinners," Petri proclaimed, "for God forgives their sins and looks upon them as good and righteous."

Eventually, the king dissolved most of the monasteries and convents in the country, and nobles claimed the land as their own. But many Swedes remained loyal to their priests and monks, and they resented the king's grasping church lands. Some bishops incited the people to rise up against Gustavus. The king's troops brutally suppressed these armed revolts.

However, over time, most nobles and peasants embraced the Evangelical faith. The church in Sweden established the Scriptures as the supreme authority for faith and practice, abolished the Latin mass in favor of worship services in Swedish and severed all ties with the Church of Rome.

Petri accepted a call to preach and teach at St. Nicholas Cathedral in the capital city, Stockholm. In addition to his preaching and writing, Petri served as a key advisor to the king. However, Petri and Gustavus often disagreed. Petri wanted confiscated church property to be used to support schools, parish churches and ministers, but Gustavus primarily used them for his own personal gain or for the benefit of his political allies. As the king grew more autocratic, he asserted his rule in the life of the church. In a proclamation to the people he wrote, "You must remain obedient to our royal commands, both in worldly things and in religious matters."

Olaf Petri insisted that the church was spiritually independent from the crown. In 1539, agents of the king arrested Petri and charged him with treason. After months of imprisonment, a court did the king's bidding and condemned him to death. But high officials of church and state petitioned the king to spare his life. Gustavus commuted the death sentence and ordered him to pay a fine. Petri returned to his preaching duties and did not shy away from proclaiming the truth of God's Word, whether it offended the king or not.

By the time of his death in 1552, most Swedes believed the doctrines that Olaf Petri preached, they read the Scriptures in Swedish that he translated, and they worshiped using the service book that he wrote.

REFORMATION BASICS 3

Sola Scriptura ("By Scripture Alone") and the Vernacular Bible

Although the Roman church of the late Middle Ages taught that the Bible was the inerrant and inspired Word of God, they placed church tradition on par with the Scriptures and declared: "No one shall presume to understand and teach the Scriptures contrary to the teachings of the holy mother Church" (Council of Trent, 1546).

Most of the forerunners of the Reformation and every one of the Protestant reformers emphasized that all the teaching that is needed for salvation is found in the Bible alone. This doctrine is known as sola Scriptura, Latin for "by Scripture alone." It means that Scripture is the supreme authority on God, the way of salvation and the Christian life. Consequently, the reformers strove to bring the Word of God to the common people by translating the Scriptures into the vernacular, the language of the people. They encouraged literacy so that members of the flock could read the Bible for themselves, and they carefully instructed their congregations in the Scriptures by preaching systematically through books of the Bible.

Priests of the Church of Rome did not teach through books of the Bible in their sermons.

Roman church officials did not encourage, and often outright banned, the translation of the Scriptures into the vernacular. They burned vernacular Bibles and persecuted men like Jacques Lefevre and William Tyndale who brought the Scriptures into the language of their countrymen.

But the reformers relied on the Bible alone as their guide to Christ. They taught their congregations to be like the Bereans described in Acts 17 who "received the word with all eagerness, examining the Scriptures daily to see if these things were so."

CHAPTER 11:
CASPER OLEVIANUS

Coauthor of the Heidelberg Catechism
(1536–1587)

In 1556, Casper Olevianus, a law student, walked along a riverside in Bourges, France, with his friend Prince Herman. Herman was the son of Elector Frederick III of the Palatinate (a region in southwestern Germany along the Rhine River). They met some of their fellow German students paddling a boat. "Hop aboard!" their friends bellowed laughingly. "Come across the river with us."

As Herman started toward the boat, Olevianus took his arm and said, "Don't go! The current is swift, and they are intoxicated."

Despite the warning, Herman climbed into the boat. When they reached the middle of the river, a few of the drunken students rocked the boat so violently that it flipped over, throwing everyone into the river. As the current dragged them downstream, the fully-clothed young men struggled to keep their heads above water. Olevianus dove into the murky river to rescue his friend, but soon he was fighting to stay afloat. Certain that he would be pulled to a watery grave, he called out in prayer, "O Lord, if You will save me from death, I will devote my life to preaching Christ in my homeland."

No sooner had he finished the prayer, then a bystander jumped in the water, grabbed the sinking Olevianus and pulled him to shore. The prince and several of the drunken students drowned.

True to his vow to God, Olevianus abandoned his law career and went to Geneva to prepare for the Christian ministry under John Calvin. After studying for two years in Switzerland, Olevianus met William Farel. He confided in the fiery, old reformer how he had vowed to preach Christ in Treves, his hometown in Germany. After Farel heard his story, he stared long into Olevianus's eyes and said, "It is your duty before God to go home and preach the gospel."

Shortly thereafter, Olevianus went to Treves and moved into his widowed mother's home. Knowing that the elector of Treves, a strident Roman Catholic, would never allow an Evangelical preacher, Olevianus did what Farel had done in Switzerland many years before, he started teaching school. The city council hired him to teach logic at a secondary school. Olevianus used Melanchthon's book on logic, filled with biblical teachings and supported by proof texts from Scripture. Day by day, he strove to lead his students to Christ.

After a few weeks, he posted a notice in the city center that he would preach the next day in German in the school auditorium. The following morning, a large crowd skipped the Latin mass to hear a sermon in their own language. Olevianus preached Christ and against devotion to saints and the sacrifice of the mass. Roman

Catholics complained about his preaching to the city council that brought him in for questioning. "My doctrine is taken only from the Word of God," he told them. "The greatest need of our fatherland is the Word of God."

Although the council forbade him from preaching at the school, the Evangelicals on the council got permission for him to preach in St. Jacob's Hospital Church, a church under the authority of the city council and not the bishop. Many came curious to hear a sermon in German and left seeking Christ. Soon the church filled to overflowing. People stood in the nave and the chancel. They sat on the pulpit steps and in the windowsills. Hundreds believed in their hearts that Christ's sacrifice reconciled them to God.

Meanwhile, leading Roman Catholics sent messages to the elector who was away at a conference, urging him to return and expel the Evangelicals. The elector denounced the Evangelicals as a "brood of vipers" and sent a demand to the city council to cast Olevianus into prison. When the city council delayed taking any action on the elector's order, the elector's council, a body chosen by the elector to oversee the spiritual affairs of Treves, banned Olevianus from preaching. However, the city council refused to arrest him or stop him from preaching.

The next day, Olevianus entered the pulpit at St. Jacob's and said, "The elector's council has banned me from preaching. You asked me to preach the eternal truth of God. If you have changed your mind, I will not preach. But if you remain steadfast to this call, I will place my life in danger in order to preach the Word of God. Those who from the heart agree to this should say 'Amen.'"

A thunderous, "Amen," erupted from the congregation. Olevianus kept preaching every day of the week to huge crowds. After just a month of his preaching, more than a quarter of the citizens declared themselves Protestants.

Before long, the elector returned to Treves with a troop of armed men, demanding that the city council arrest Olevianus. When they refused and barred the city gates to his soldiers, the elector's forces prevented food shipments into Treves, and they burned fields outside the city to starve the citizens into submission. Eventually, the city council relented and permitted the troops to enter. They arrested Olevianus and the leading Evangelicals on the council and charged them with treason and heresy, crimes punishable by death.

Frederick, the elector of the Palatinate, sent representatives to Treves to intercede on behalf of the Evangelicals and so did other Protestant German princes. The elector of Treves agreed to drop the criminal charges against the Protestants, if they paid a fine and left the city forever. All the Evangelicals agreed to the terms except Olevianus. "I cannot pay anything, as I have nothing," he said. He filed a protest, contesting the charges against him.

When they released Olevianus after ten weeks in prison, he accepted an invitation from Frederick to come to Heidelberg. Ever grateful for Olevianus's heroic effort to save his son's life, Frederick appointed Olevianus professor of theology in the university and court preacher. Olevianus used his influence to promote Reformed theology——the teachings of the Scriptures by the Swiss reformers, especially John Calvin. Critics branded Reformed theology "Calvinism." Frederick also hired Zacharias Ursinus, a brilliant scholar, to teach theology at the University of Heidelberg. Under the influence of Olevianus and Ursinus, Frederick embraced Reformed theology which differed from the teachings of Luther and Melanchthon in some areas, especially in respect to worship and the Lord's Supper.

When Frederick dissolved monasteries and other properties once held by the Church of Rome, he did not do as Henry VIII and other Protestant monarchs had done. They confiscated church wealth for themselves or for their aristocratic friends. Instead, Frederick devoted the money to endow churches, schools, poor houses and hospitals. When asked why he did not use some of the resources to build forts, Frederick replied, "A mighty fortress is our God."

In 1562, Frederick commissioned twenty-six-year-old Olevianus and twenty-eight-year-old Ursinus to head a team of ministers to write a catechism to unite his subjects in their understanding of Christ and the sacraments. The two men brought unique gifts to the task, Olevianus's command of the German language and a knack for expressing ideas eloquently and Ursinus's strong scholarship and deep knowledge of the Scriptures. Unlike the catechisms written by Luther, Calvin and others that were organized around subjects like the Lord's Prayer and the Ten Commandments, Olevianus and Ursinus took a different approach. Their catechism explains the Christian message as a unified whole, detailing God's grace in the heart of a believer from the conviction of sin to trusting Christ to living a thankful, obedient life. The grace of God in Christ is its central theme. Written in the first person, it exudes a warm and joyful personal trust in Jesus Christ from the first question and answer to the last. And they supplied many Scripture references to support each answer.

Question 1: What is your only comfort in life and death?

Answer: That I am not my own, but belong—body and soul, in life and in death— to my faithful Savior Jesus Christ. He has fully paid for all my sins with His precious blood, and has set me free from the tyranny of the devil. He also watches over me in such a way that not a hair can fall from my head without the will of my Father in heaven: in fact, all things must work together for my salvation. Because

I belong to Him, Christ, by His Holy Spirit, assures me of eternal life and makes me wholeheartedly willing and ready from now on to live for Him.

The completed catechism was quickly adopted as a confession of faith in the Palatinate. But as soon as Frederick commissioned the publication of the Heidelberg Catechism, it caused an uproar in the German states of the Holy Roman Empire. The Peace of Augsburg in 1555 allowed German states to be Lutheran——those who accepted the Augsburg Confession——or Roman Catholic, if their prince so chose. It did not make allowances for the Reformed faith. Emperor Maximilian called for a diet of the German states, hoping to persuade the German princes to depose Frederick and overthrow the Reformed faith in the Palatinate. Knowing the grave danger he faced, Frederick contacted the Protestant princes and explained to them all that the Reformed and the Lutherans held in common regarding the essential doctrines of Christianity. He urged them to stand united to prevent the Roman Catholic princes and the emperor from driving a wedge between them, but he found little encouragement.

When Frederick arrived at the diet, he expected to defend himself against the charges made against him. Instead, the emperor informed him that he would be deposed if he did not immediately suppress the Heidelberg Catechism and banish Calvinism from his realm. Frederick protested that it violated German custom to be condemned unheard. Several Protestant princes insisted that Frederick be allowed to present his defense, and the emperor reluctantly agreed.

Frederick stood erect before the diet and said, "I confess freely that in those things which concern the conscience, I acknowledge as Master only the Lord of Lords and King of Kings. For the question here pertains to the soul and its salvation, for which I am indebted alone to my Lord and Savior Jesus Christ as His gift. Therefore, I cannot grant your imperial majesty the right of standing in the place of my God and Savior."

All was quiet as Frederick continued. "What men understand by Calvinism I do not know," he said. "But the Augsburg Confession that I signed together with the other princes here present, in this faith I continue firmly because I find it established in the holy Scriptures of the Old and New Testaments. My catechism, word for word, is drawn not from human but from divine sources, as the Scripture references show. If anyone can teach me something better from the holy Scriptures, I will thank him from the bottom of my heart and readily obey the divine truth. If there is anyone here among my lords and friends who will undertake it, I am prepared to hear him."

Frederick paused and looked around the assembly, but no one spoke or offered to teach him from the Scriptures. Then Frederick said, "I shall comfort myself in this, that my Lord and Savior Jesus Christ has promised to me and to all who believe that whatsoever we lose on earth for His name's sake, we shall receive a hundredfold in the life to come."

The speech deeply affected the assembly. The elector of Saxony leapt to his feet, clapped Frederick on the back and said, "Fritz, you are more pious than all of us." Another member said, "Why do we attack this prince, when he is more devout than we are?"

The Protestant princes refused to take any action against him. Frederick had preserved the Heidelberg Catechism and prevented religious interference from the emperor in the Palatinate. He returned home to great rejoicing, for the people had heard rumors that he had been deposed and even beheaded.

For the next ten years, Frederick worked with Olevianus and Ursinus to expand the Evangelical faith in the Palatinate and beyond. In time, the Protestants of the Netherlands and a number of German cities and provinces adopted the Heidelberg Catechism. It was translated into nearly all the languages of Europe. Through the centuries it has been praised as one of the warmest and most beautiful expressions of the Christian faith.

When Frederick died in 1576, he was succeeded by his son Louis, a high-church Lutheran who disliked Reformed theology. He banished Olevianus and hundreds of other Reformed ministers from the land. Olevianus accepted a position as a tutor to the sons of a German nobleman. Later, he started a seminary to prepare young men for the ministry.

At the age of fifty, he fell ill with the sickness that would take his life. As Olevianus lay on his deathbed, someone asked him, "Are you certain of your salvation?"

"Most certain!" Olevianus answered.

CHAPTER 12:
WILLIAM THE SILENT,
PRINCE OF ORANGE

Defender of the Dutch Protestants

(1533–1584)

I n 1559, Philip II, King of Spain and ruler of the Netherlands, sent Prince William of Orange to Paris. William, an important leader in the Netherlands, acted as a representative of Philip's government in negotiations with King Henry II of France. One day, Henry brought the twenty-six-year-old William with him on a hunting party. As they rode along on horseback, Henry——supposing that William was in the full confidence of King Philip—told William the details of a secret plot between himself and Philip to wipe out the Evangelicals in France and the Netherlands. "We shall," Henry said, "exterminate heresy by exterminating heretics!"

Henry told William that Philip planned to use his Spanish troops stationed in the Netherlands to massacre Protestants.

When William heard that Philip intended to kill the unsuspecting Dutch Protestants, his heart leapt in his chest and his hands trembled at the reins. It was all he could do to keep himself from crying out in horror at the news. But he held his tongue and did not let on to Henry his shock and anger. "I was moved by pity and compassion for so many worthy people doomed to slaughter," William said later. "I determined to drive those Spanish vermin from the country." For keeping quiet at that crucial moment, he later became known as "William the Silent."

At that time, William considered himself a faithful Roman Catholic. During his early boyhood living in Germany, his mother raised him in the Evangelical faith. But at age eleven, William inherited from his cousin vast lands in the Netherlands. As a condition of inheriting the land, Emperor Charles V, Philip II's father, insisted that William be raised Roman Catholic in his court in Madrid.

A few days after William learned of the plan to kill Protestants, he returned to the Netherlands. Racing from city to city, he warned nobles and magistrates of the murderous plot and urged them to protect the people. "We must at all costs remove the Spanish troops from the land."

In August 1559, Philip II asked the assembly of the Netherlands to grant him a large sum of money. Philip was not the absolute ruler of the Netherlands as he was in Spain. The Dutch constitutions limited his powers. With William's warning ringing in their ears, the assembly told Philip that they would provide the money only after he removed all Spanish troops from the land. Philip's blood boiled at this demand, even though it was within their rights to do so, and he blamed William for it.

Eventually, Philip withdrew most of the Spanish troops from the Netherlands, but he kept some of them in place to enforce the Inquisition——an illegal tribunal used to stamp out the Evangelical faith. "I would carry the wood to burn my own son," Philip said, "if he was infected with Lutheran errors. I would rather be a king without subjects than a ruler over heretics."

The Spanish inquisitors tortured Protestant preachers and laymen and burned many at the stake. William pled with Philip and his representatives to respect the rights of the Netherlanders. "I cannot look on with pleasure," William wrote to Philip, "when princes strive to govern the souls of men and to take away their liberty in matters of conscience and religion."

Despite the persecution, many people stopped looking to Mary, the saints and the parish priest to intercede for them with God and put their trust in Christ alone. In every province, thousands flocked to the fields to hear Evangelical preachers who were banned from the churches. The king's regent in the Netherlands offered a large reward for the capture of any field preacher——dead or alive. When a group of Evangelical nobles came and petitioned the regent for redress, a high official interrupted them and said, "Must your highness listen to these beggars?"

The petitioners took up the name "beggars" as a badge of honor. Soon the cry, "Long live the beggars!" echoed over the land.

Across the Netherlands, the people vented their anger with the Roman church and the Inquisition by bursting into churches and smashing statues that they believed encouraged idolatry. William deplored their unruly and destructive conduct. He demanded an end to the riotous behavior and warned that such actions would destroy the reputation of Protestants and bring down more of Philip's wrath.

In 1567, Philip——fed up with the unrest in the Netherlands——made the Duke of Alva the Governor-General of the Netherlands. Alva invaded with an army of 10,000 battle-hardened Spanish soldiers. Sweeping aside the historic privileges of the provincial assemblies, he ruled through a tribunal empowered to condemn without trial people suspected of disloyalty or heresy. "I will hang every man in the country," Alva said, "for his Majesty would rather the whole land should become an uninhabited wilderness than a single Protestant should exist within its territory."

Alva demanded that Prince William and other leading nobles appear before his tribunal. William refused to recognize Alva as the legitimate governor of the Netherlands, and he advised the nobles to boycott the tribunal. Many of those who ignored his advice and appeared before Alva were arrested and executed. When William fled the country to the safety of his lands in Germany, Alva declared him an outlaw and confiscated all his property for the crown.

People suspected of rebellion or heresy were snatched from their homes, cast into prison and tortured. Spanish authorities hanged, burned or drowned thousands of Evangelicals for their faith. To prevent the condemned prisoners from speaking to the crowds at their executions, guards seared their tongues with a hot iron. They burned a man at the stake for hand-copying hymns from a Reformed worship book and put to death a woman for reading the Scriptures in her home. Anyone who refused to attend Roman Catholic services could face fire and the sword. The executions and the brutality of the Spanish soldiers marauding through the countryside turned the people against Philip's rule.

In Germany, William reexamined his faith. He studied the Scriptures and read books by Luther and Melanchthon and brought an Evangelical minister to preach in his palace. Soon

William accepted Christ with a believing heart and returned to the Protestant faith of his deceased parents. "I give thanks to God," he said, "who did not permit this holy seed which He Himself planted in me to be choked."

Meanwhile, William used his wealth to support the Dutch Evangelicals. Holland and Zeeland——northern provinces with the largest number of Evangelicals——asked William to lead their fight against the Spanish. William tried to convince German Protestant princes to send troops to support the Evangelicals of the Netherlands, but they counseled William to "sit still and wait." Unwilling to sit still while the people of the Netherlands suffered, he raised a 30,000-man army of German soldiers and French Huguenots and marched into the Netherlands. Alva knew that if William won a victory, nearly all the people would rally to William's banner, so Alva ordered his troops not to engage them in battle. After weeks of chasing the elusive Spanish army, William had to release his foreign soldiers because he could not afford to feed and pay them any longer.

When William's army disbanded, Alva unleashed a brutal rampage across the northern provinces, overrunning and plundering cities and towns. In Naarden, the citizens negotiated a peaceful surrender. But when the Spanish troops entered the city, they forced the 3,000 townspeople into a church, bolted the doors and burned it to the ground. Next, they lay siege to Haarlem which held out behind their city walls for eight months until starvation forced them to surrender. The Spaniards put to death the Dutch soldiers in the town and all the members of the city council. Although victories on land were few, the Sea Beggars——the ragtag Dutch naval force—— won many victories at sea, snatching stores of food and valuables from Spanish ships.

William set up headquarters in Rotterdam, Holland, and organized the Dutch resistance to Alva. In the cities under Dutch control, William insisted on freedom of worship for the citizens——even Roman Catholics who supported Philip's reign. "See that the Word of God is preached without hindering the Roman church in the exercise of its religion," William ordered the magistrates. He wanted the Netherlands to respect the freedom of conscience for Roman Catholics, Reformed Protestants, Lutherans and Anabaptists. His thinking on religious liberty was far ahead of his time and was not accepted by most Dutch leaders.

Much of Holland lies below sea level. Over many centuries, the industrious Hollanders reclaimed the land from the sea by building a network of dikes to hold back the ocean. In 1573, the Spanish lay siege to the city of Leiden, an important walled city about 15 miles inland from the coast. As the siege dragged on for months, the daily ration of food grew smaller and smaller. The beleaguered citizens communicated with William by carrier pigeon, sending heart-wrenching notes describing their plight and begging William for relief. The people survived on any green leaves they could find, and they resorted to eating rats, cats and dogs. Disease swept through the malnourished population, killing 8,000 men, women and children.

To break the siege, William won the approval of the provincial assembly to breach the dikes and flood the countryside. "Better a drowned land than a lost land," the representatives told him. This would destroy tens of thousands of acres of field crops and orchards. Dike after dike were breached and the waters crept over the land, but the Spanish had strong forts guarding some key dikes nearest the city. The flooding enabled the Sea Beggars' ships to sail to the outskirts of Leiden, and they prepared for a deadly fight against the Spanish garrison.

The night of October 2, 1574, the Spaniards heard a thunderous crash. Thinking that the Dutch were storming their position, they lit torches and slipped away before sunrise. In the morning, the townspeople discovered that the loud sound came when a section of the city wall fell over. If the Spanish had realized it, they could have rushed into the defenseless city. Food supplies poured in to the great relief of the starving townspeople. When William visited Leiden a few days later, the people crowded around their leader cheering, "Father William, Father William!"

In April 1575, Holland and Zeeland united, and they asked William to govern their nation with the elected assemblies. "If the remainder of my property and my life can be of service to you," William said, "I dedicate them afresh to you and to the country." Under his leadership, they battled for years with the Spanish troops who remained determined to oppress them. He worked hard to gain the support of England and the Protestant states of Germany, but their support was often unreliable. "Even if the entire world turns against us," William told the people, "we shall not cease to defend ourselves even to the last man. Knowing the justice of our cause we rest entirely on the mercy of God."

Philip II knew that William's strong leadership stiffened the resolve of the Dutch people to defend themselves. So he offered a reward of 25,000 gold crowns to any man who assassinated Prince William. When William learned of the price on his head, he said, "I am in the hand of God. My worldly goods and my life have been long since dedicated to His service. He will dispose of them as seems best for His glory and for my salvation."

Five different times assassins attempted to murder William. Once, he was shot in the head, but remarkably, he survived. But in July 1584, an assassin shot William in the heart. He slumped to the floor and cried out, "O my God, have mercy upon my soul! O my God, have mercy upon this people!"

As William lay dying, his sister asked him, "Do you commend your soul to Jesus Christ?"

"Yes," he answered with his last breath.

The struggle with Spain continued for decades, but eventually Spain had to recognize an independent Dutch republic. It became a haven for Protestant refugees fleeing religious persecution. The English nonconformists——known to us as the Pilgrim Fathers—— found freedom to worship God in the Netherlands. From there, they crossed the Atlantic on the *Mayflower* and established Plymouth Colony in the Massachusetts wilderness.

William the Silent's great personal sacrifice on behalf of civil liberties and religious freedoms shines as a beacon of light to this day.

COMPREHENSION QUESTIONS

for Part Two

1. Why did the fact that Luther lived in Saxony, Germany, help him to promote the Reformation?

2. Why was Luther angry about the sale of indulgences?

3. Did Luther plan to start the Reformation when he posted the Ninety-five Theses?

4. Why did Luther refuse to recant his views at the Diet of Worms?

5. Who were Hendrich Voes and Johann Esch?

6. Contrast the personalities and styles of Luther and Melanchthon.

7. What were Melanchthon's great contributions to the Reformation?

8. How did Martin Bucer come to a living faith in Christ?

9. What did Bucer strive throughout his lifetime to do with the other reformers?

10. Why is Katherine Zell called the "Mother of the Reformers?"

11. In what ways did Olaf Petri help to advance the Reformation in Sweden?

12. What was the greatest way that Casper Olevianus promoted the Reformed faith?

13. How did William the Silent get his nickname?

14. Why was William the Silent, Prince of Orange, so revered by the Dutch Protestants?

PART THREE

THE REFORMATION
IN FRANCE,
SWITZERLAND
AND ITALY

At the same time that Luther proclaimed justification by faith alone in Germany, Ulrich Zwingli in Switzerland came to the same doctrine through his own study of the Scriptures. He preached in Zurich and before long that influential canton embraced the Reformation. Other Swiss city-states soon followed. In France, Jacques Lefevre's translation of the New Testament into French and the preaching of Evangelical ministers led thousands of their countrymen to trust in Christ. But officials of the French church and state unleashed a bitter persecution that drove reformers like William Farel and John Calvin to flee to Switzerland for safety. The persecution of French Protestants gave rise to civil wars that ravaged the country for decades. Calvin's work in Geneva transformed the city. It became the most influential center in Europe for the Protestant Reformation. Sadly, differences of opinion about the Lord's Supper separated Luther and the German Protestants from Zwingli and Calvin and the other Swiss and French Evangelicals.

CHAPTER 13:
JACQUES LEFEVRE

The Spark of the French Reformation
(c.1450–1536)

One day around the year 1507, Jacques Lefevre, a professor at the Sorbonne, the theological college of the University of Paris, unwittingly took the first step of the Protestant Reformation. For years, he had painstakingly collected the stories of the saints of the Church of Rome. He planned to write a multi-volume work, detailing the lives of all the saints in the church's calendar of feast days. When Lefevre wasn't lecturing or writing, he spent hours visiting shrines to the saints and Mary, decorating the images with flowers and imploring the saints for help. But then one day, almost on a whim, Lefevre set aside his great project and picked up the Scriptures.

Although Lefevre was nearly sixty years old and had served for years as a professor of theology, he had never carefully studied the

Scriptures for himself. Now, he began to examine the gospels and the letters of the New Testament. He quickly recognized the great gulf that separated the simple, yet powerful, accounts of the life of Christ found in the gospels with the fanciful tales of the saints. Lefevre gave every spare minute to studying the New Testament. With Scripture enlightening his mind, he saw that all his zeal to venerate relics and pray to the saints could never bring him peace with God. "It is God alone," he said, "who, by His grace, through faith, justifies unto everlasting life. The righteousness of works comes from man and is earthly and passes away. The righteousness of grace comes from God and is heavenly and eternal."

Lefevre had rediscovered the biblical doctrine of justification by faith that had been lost for centuries——and he was a new man. He stopped looking to religious rituals to be made right with God and looked only to Christ for saving mercy and the grace to obey His commands. And he started to teach others what he had discovered in the Bible. "The cross of Christ alone opens heaven and shuts the gates of hell," he said. One of his students, William Farel, admired Lefevre and used to worship with him at the shrines of Paris. "God will renew the world, and you will see it," Lefevre told Farel. "Soon, God will give us new light by His Holy Spirit. The Word of God will take the place of the word of the church. We must give up the lives of the saints and read the words of the apostles."

"But aren't you going to publish the lives of the saints?" Farel asked.

"No," Lefevre answered, "I began the task with zeal, but I am weary of them. They disgust me. They are foolish legends at best—— childish superstitions——kindling for the fire of idolatry. They cause us to idolize the saints and to neglect our Lord. They are paltry fables that keep us from the sublime Word of God."

"How did you come to learn this so suddenly?" Farel asked.

"By one of those beams of light which comes from heaven through the Holy Spirit," Lefevre answered. "I was struck with the blasphemy of addressing prayers to the saints. Go, dear William, to the Bible."

"But don't the saints help to lift our prayers to God?" Farel asked.

"My dear son," Lefevre told him, "we cannot be sure that the saints hear any words we speak. We know they cannot hear different persons in different places at the same time. We are sure that Jesus, the Father and the Holy Spirit do hear us, and we should pray only to this holy Trinity."

"But," Farel said, "the saints have such feeling for us."

"Jesus has infinitely more," Lefevre replied. "He is touched with the feeling of our weaknesses. He knows us altogether. No saint can have such a tender sympathy for us as Christ. He, only, is the head of the church. Let the servant pray only to the Master. Our prayers must reach the willing ear of God, or they are useless. Let them go up directly to Him."

"After that," Farel said later, "the holy Word of God had the chief place in my heart."

In class lectures and private conversations, Lefevre spread the good news of peace with God and new life through Jesus Christ, the friend of sinners. "Free grace is offered to us in Christ," he proclaimed. Lefevre marveled at the unfathomable sacrifice of Christ for sinners on the cross and tried to help others see it too. "How indescribably amazing!" he preached. "The Innocent One is condemned and the criminal acquitted. The Blessed One is cursed, and he who was cursed is blessed."

In 1512, Lefevre published a commentary on the Apostle Paul's New Testament letters. It was widely read and discussed in the universities and monasteries of Europe. "God, in His great mercy,"

Lefevre wrote, "will soon revive the dying spark in the hearts of men, so that faith and love and a purer worship will return."

Many people rejoiced to learn about the grace of God's forgiveness in Jesus Christ. Others complained that it went against the teachings of the Church of Rome. "Lefevre's doctrine of salvation by grace as a free gift from God will destroy morality and the foundation of good works," argued some professors of the Sorbonne. "The Apostle James taught righteousness by good works," they claimed.

"Does not James in his first chapter declare that every good and perfect gift comes down from above?" Lefevre asked, as he reasoned with his critics. "Now who will deny that justification is that good and perfect gift? Works are necessary, but only as signs of a living faith, which follow justification."

Far from dismissing holy living, Lefevre called his hearers to love and thank Christ by obeying His commandments. "Your lives are hid with Christ in God," he preached. "Oh! If men could only understand this privilege, what chaste, pure and holy lives they would live."

Lefevre called on the priests and bishops to teach the people the Word of God and put away their scandalous lives. They will not lead them to Jesus Christ, Lefevre complained, but they will "ask them to join them in drinking, gambling, hawking and frequenting the worst houses and haunts."

A growing circle of students, professors and citizens of Paris embraced Lefevre's teaching. Even many churchmen believed that Christ fully paid for all their sins on the cross. Among them was Briconnet, the bishop of Meaux, a city a day's ride east of Paris. "I am in darkness," Briconnet told Lefevre, "a stranger to divine goodness because of my sins."

"Get into your heart more of that good Bible," Lefevre told him. "It will give you light. It will lead you back to the purer Christianity of the early church."

When Briconnet searched the Scriptures, he found forgiveness in Christ and began a close personal relationship with his Savior. "Such is the sweetness of this divine food," Briconnet said of the Bible, "the more we taste it, the more we long for." He returned to his diocese, urging his priests to teach their parishioners the Word of God, calling them to embrace Christ and turn from their sins.

Queen Margaret of Navarre,* the sister of King Francis I of France, read Lefevre's books with eagerness. She visited Lefevre to learn the Scriptures from him, and she told Francis what Lefevre had taught her of Christ. Leaders of the French church and the Sorbonne—shocked by Lefevre's growing influence among the people and in the royal court—lashed out at him. They accused him of heresy, even though he had never questioned the authority of the pope or the central teachings of the Roman church. After a sham trial, the Sorbonne and the French parliament condemned Lefevre to death as a heretic. But Francis intervened and saved him from execution.

The University of Paris was in an uproar over Lefevre's teaching. If the king refused to arrest and burn Lefevre, then his enemies in the university and the church would hound him into silence. They interrupted his lectures with shouts and spread slanderous lies about him. The tormented Lefevre found it impossible to do his work. Bishop Briconnet invited him to Meaux. Other Evangelicals were harassed and imprisoned. Some died at the stake.

Living under the bishop's protection at Meaux, Lefevre helped to train pastors, and he undertook his most ambitious project of

---

* Read about Margaret of Navarre in *Radiant: Fifty Remarkable Women in Church History* (2015).

all——translating the Scriptures into French. Lefevre wanted every man and woman, rich and poor, in France to read the Bible in their own language. Within three years, he completed his translation of the entire New Testament. It was published in 1523 and was eagerly purchased across the kingdom. "Nations awake to the light of the gospel and inhale the heavenly life," Lefevre proclaimed. "The Word of God is all sufficient."

In Meaux——through the encouragement of Bishop Bricon-net——shopkeepers, farmers and milkmaids read the New Testament for themselves, and shared what they learned with their neighbors. "As they work with their hands, they talk with each other about the Word of God," one man observed. "Sundays and holidays are devoted to the reading of Scripture and seeking the good pleasure of the Lord."

"The gospel is gaining the hearts of the high and low," Lefevre said. "In a short time, spreading all over France, it will everywhere throw down the inventions of man."

But leaders of the French church and government officials had no intention of allowing that to happen. "Does Lefevre dare to recommend all the faithful to read the Scripture?" They asked. "Does he dare to teach that the Word of God is sufficient to lead to eternal life?"

The Sorbonne and parliament condemned Lefevre's teachings and banned his French New Testament. They demanded that Bri-connet stop harboring Lefevre and other Evangelicals. "Crush this heresy," they told Briconnet, "or else the pestilence which is already destroying the city of Meaux will spread over the kingdom."

Under heavy pressure, Bishop Briconnet submitted, but he refused to allow Lefevre to be arrested. He helped him flee to Stras-bourg. Eventually, Lefevre found sanctuary in the Kingdom of

Navarre under the protection of Queen Margaret. Other reformers found their way to Navarre. Among them was John Calvin who longed to meet the aged Lefevre whose French New Testament had been such a blessing to him. "Young man," Lefevre told Calvin, "you will one day be a powerful instrument in the Lord's hand. God will use you to restore the kingdom of heaven to France. Be on your guard and let your ardor be always tempered with charity."

In exile, Lefevre completed a French translation of the whole Bible. It was printed in Switzerland and smuggled into France. His masterful translation was eloquent enough to be appreciated by the educated elite and simple enough to be understood by the unschooled.

Although Lefevre encouraged staunch reformers like Farel and Calvin, he remained loyal to the Church of Rome—accepting the authority of the pope and the doctrines of purgatory and the sacrifice of the mass. Not long before he died, as Queen Margaret visited him, Lefevre burst into tears. "What is wrong?" Margaret asked. He told her that he reproached himself for failing to be bolder in the cause of Christ. "I should have died a martyr's death," he said.

However, Lefevre's teaching about the grace of God and his translation of the Scriptures into French sparked a great awakening of faith in Christ in France, Switzerland and beyond. As one church historian put it, "The moment when Lefevre quit the marvelous tales of the saints and laid his hand on the Word of God was the beginning of the Reformation in France."

CHAPTER 14:
ULRICH ZWINGLI

Father of the Swiss Reformation
(1484 –1531)

In December 1518, Ulrich Zwingli, a thirty-four-year-old preacher, stood before the canons, the church officials in charge of the great cathedral in Zurich, Switzerland. They had recently chosen Zwingli to be the cathedral preacher. "Welcome, Master Zwingli," the chief canon said. "We pray that God will bless your ministry here. We want you to make every effort to bring in money. You will exhort the faithful——both from the pulpit and in the confessional——to pay all tithes and dues. You must work to increase the income from every church service."

Zwingli had no intention of being the kind of preacher that these men wanted. Ignoring their advice, he said, "I thank you for your call to be the cathedral preacher. The life of Christ has been too long hidden from the people. I shall preach upon the whole Gospel of Matthew, chapter by chapter, drawing solely from the fountains of Scripture and seeking understanding by constant and earnest prayer. I shall devote my ministry to God's glory and the praise of His only Son and to the real salvation of souls."

The shocked canons looked at one another in disbelief. They were used to reading a few lines of Scripture in Latin and had never encountered systematic preaching through whole books of the Bible. Some of the canons looked forward to this new approach, but others dreaded any thought of straying from the old paths. "This explanation of Scripture will be more harmful than helpful to the people," one said.

"This way of preaching is an innovation," another complained. "One new plan will lead to another and where will it stop?"

"This is not a new way," Zwingli replied. "It is the old custom. The church father Chrysostom preached through the Gospel of Matthew, and Augustine preached all of the Gospel of John."

On Saturday, January 1, 1519, Zwingli entered Zurich's cathedral pulpit for the first time. A large crowd came out to see him. "It is to Christ that I desire to lead you," he told them, "to Christ the true source of salvation. His divine word is the only food that I wish to set before your souls. Starting on the Lord's Day tomorrow, I will begin to preach through the Gospel of Matthew line by line."

Sunday morning, people filled the cathedral to hear the new preacher. With his Greek New Testament opened before him, he preached in German, the language of the people. He used words that all could understand. And he preached with heart. "He was named Jesus," he told them, "because Jesus means 'God is salvation.' Jesus came to save His people from their sins. Christ is your righteousness. Christ is your salvation. You are nothing, you can do nothing, but Christ is all, and He can do everything."

"We never heard anything like this before," the people said to one another as they left the service.

A few years earlier, when Zwingli served at the abbey church in Einsiedeln, he found a living faith in Christ by reading the New Testament in Greek. "I came to rely on no single word," Zwingli said, "save that which came from the mouth of the Lord. I now began to subject every doctrine to the test of Scripture." He started to memorize Scripture. Over time, he knew the gospels and all of Paul's letters by heart. The more he studied the Word of God, the clearer he saw that many of the beliefs and practices of the Roman church could not be supported by Scripture. And some of the worst abuses were on display at Einsiedeln Abbey. For centuries, pilgrims from every country in Europe had streamed to the abbey to adore an image of the Virgin Mary that was said to have miraculous powers. A sign above the abbey gate read: "Here you may obtain a full remission of all sins." The pilgrims gave money at the Virgin's shrine and prayed for her blessing. Zwingli's heart went out to these poor misguided folks. "Look to Christ!" he told them. "Christ offered himself once for all on the cross and made satisfaction forever for the sins of all the faithful."

Zwingli explained to them that God's blessing did not rest in a particular place or in images made by human hands. "Do not imagine that God is in this temple more than in any other part of His creation," he said. "He is in your country, and He can hear and help you. Pilgrimages, offerings, images, the invocation of saints or Mary cannot bring to you the grace of God. Christ alone saves, and He saves everywhere."

"If you wish to specially honor Mary," Zwingli said, "then follow her purity and faith." Many of the pilgrims turned away from the image of Mary and put their faith in Jesus Christ alone. They went home telling others what they had learned. Zwingli persuaded the abbot to remove the sign over the abbey gate, and each year fewer and fewer pilgrims arrived to pay homage to the Virgin Mary there. Some of the monks at Einsiedeln Abbey resented Zwingli's preaching and lamented the loss of the pilgrims' money, but others rejoiced to find true faith in Christ.

When Zwingli went to Zurich from Einsiedeln, he began to learn Hebrew so that he could read the Old Testament in its original language. Rising before dawn each day, he spent several hours in prayer and Bible study and sermon preparation——preferring to study and write standing up. In the afternoon, he went out among the people and talked to shopkeepers and laborers. In the evening, he resumed his studies and wrote letters until midnight. On Fridays, Zwingli preached to the peasants who came to sell their produce at the farmers' market.

More than two thousand people listened to his sermons every week, and they grew hungrier for the meat of God's Word. Visitors from other Swiss cantons heard him preach and brought the message back to their communities. Besides his preaching, Zwingli wrote books about Christ and faith. His printed sermons and books led other Swiss towns to embrace the Evangelical faith. "All Switzerland hears you," a friend of Zwingli told him.

The labors of Zwingli's first year in Zurich left him sick and totally exhausted. His friends convinced him to go to a mineral spring for a few weeks to heal and rest. While he was away, he got news that a plague had swept across Zurich, killing many people. "Stay away," his friends advised him, "guard your own life." But Zwingli rushed back to comfort the sick and dying. He caught the disease and lay on his bed near death. As the plague ran its course, it killed one out of every four people in Zurich. After several weeks of barely clinging to life, Zwingli recovered.

Soon, he resumed his busy schedule of study, prayer and preaching. With renewed passion, he challenged his hearers not to trust in their own good works, or in the saints, or in pardons from the pope, but in Christ alone for mercy. "The sum of the gospel," he said, "is that Christ has redeemed us from eternal death and reconciled us to God."

During the next few years, Zwingli preached through most of the books of the New Testament, and thousands received the gift of Christ with a believing heart——citizens of Zurich and visitors alike. Zwingli rejoiced saying, "Those who once were in darkness now have the blazing light of God's truth."

Zurich and other Swiss cities held debates about reforming the church. Zwingli became the chief spokesman for the Reformation. Enemies of reform claimed that the old ways of the church——the Latin mass, prayers to saints, images and relics——all communicated God's truth to the common people. "Worthy citizens," Zwingli replied, "there is another way besides these vain practices. We can lead the simple people to the knowledge of the truth of Christ in the gospel itself! Let us not fear that the people cannot understand it——whoever believes understands. In every nation, whoever believes with his heart in Jesus Christ is saved."

Zwingli excelled in debate by using the Scriptures and the writings of the early church fathers to point audiences to Christ. People from across Switzerland attended these public discussions. Many priests and laymen returned to their churches convinced that the Word of God should be their only source for faith and life. Defenders of the Roman church branded Zwingli a heretic and said, "He is disturbing the peace of Switzerland."

Once, a Franciscan friar was preaching in Zurich while Zwingli sat in the congregation. When the friar encouraged the people to pray to Mary and the saints, Zwingli called out, "Brother, you are wrong!" The friar challenged Zwingli to a public debate on the matter. The next day, the two men debated whether Christians should pray to the saints or not. Zwingli demonstrated from many passages in the Old and New Testaments that believers are never encouraged to pray to anyone other than God Himself. The friar quoted the writings of church theologians in support of praying to saints, but he admitted that the Scriptures do not teach it. Finally, after four hours of discussion, the friar clasped his hands and prayed aloud, "O Lord, I thank You that You have used this good man to give me clearer knowledge of the truth." Then he turned to the audience and said, "From now on I will pray to God only."

However, while Zwingli made friends for Christ, he also made many enemies. "Be on your guard," a friend warned him, "for on every side you are surrounded by traps and snares ready to take you away." Several times, rock throwers broke out the windows of his house. Once, a group of men tried to lure Zwingli from his home at night to kill him. Later, his foes hatched a plot to poison him. Through it all, Zwingli pressed on. "True soldiers of Christ are not afraid to bear their master's wounds in their own bodies," he said. "I labor to lead all men to the only true God and to Jesus Christ His Son."

Eventually, the city magistrates in Zurich enacted a decree that called on all priests to preach the good news of Christ and teach only what they could prove by the Word of God. Before long, they broke away from the authority of the pope in Rome. They exchanged the Latin mass for a worship service in German, abandoned prayers to saints, removed images and replaced stone altars with wooden tables for celebrating the Lord's Supper.

While all this was happening in Switzerland, Luther led the Reformation in Germany. A powerful German nobleman, Philip of

Hesse, worried that the emperor or the king of France might try to crush the Reformation by force. He wanted to unify the Swiss and German reformers for mutual protection. Philip brought Luther and the German reformers and Zwingli and the Swiss reformers to his castle in Marburg for a meeting. As they consulted with one another, they agreed on all the essential truths of the Christian faith, but they could not agree on the Lord's Supper. Luther insisted that Christ was physically present in the bread and wine. Zwingli argued that the Supper served as a memorial of Christ's death on the cross and that Christ was not physically present in the elements. When it became clear that they could not agree on the sacrament, Philip of Hesse said, "Sirs, you cannot leave like this." He begged them to come together as brothers. Then Zwingli arose—and with tears brimming in his eyes—said, "Let us confess our union in all things in which we agree and as for the rest, let us remember that we are brothers. There is no one on earth with whom I more desire to be united than with you."

Then Zwingli stood before Luther with his hand outstretched in brotherly friendship. But Luther refused to shake his hand, saying, "You have a different spirit from ours. We cannot acknowledge you as brothers." Despite all they held in common, the reformers left the meeting divided.

The great awakening of faith in Christ and the rejection of the Church of Rome by Zurich and several other Swiss cantons inflamed tensions in Switzerland. The cantons that clung to the Roman church formed a military alliance against Zurich and its allies. Zurich unwisely imposed an economic blockade on some of the Catholic cantons that inflicted great hardships upon them. In October 1531, they declared war on Zurich. Zwingli went out with the troops as a field chaplain, dressed for war and carrying a battle ax.

Zurich suffered a crushing defeat. Hundreds of soldiers lay dead on the battlefield, including Ulrich Zwingli.

The Swiss Reformation did not die with Zwingli. In the years that followed, the seeds planted by Zwingli led to a great harvest of souls as more and more Swiss repented of their sins and turned to Christ through the preaching and teaching of Henry Bullinger and John Calvin and others. And the Evangelical cities of Switzerland became havens of refuge for persecuted Protestants from across Europe.

REFORMATION BASICS 4

Purgatory and Indulgences

During the Middle Ages, the Church of Rome began to teach that Christ's death on the cross did not fully pay the penalty for His people's sin, but that believers must still be purged of their sins after death by a long period of punishment in a place called purgatory to make them fit for heaven. Although purgatory cannot be found in the Bible——the Scriptures reveal that there are only two destinies after death, heaven or hell——the medieval church made the doctrine of purgatory an important part of its teaching about salvation and eternal life.

The church also declared that the living could reduce the time of suffering of their relatives and friends in purgatory through prayer, having masses offered on their behalf and by buying indulgences. An indulgence could be granted by the pope to remit part of the punishment that souls suffer in purgatory. The doctrine of purgatory became a powerful fundraising instrument for the church. Nobles bequeathed vast sums in their wills to monasteries and churches in order that priests might say masses on their behalf to shorten their time in purgatory. Indulgence salesmen——endorsed by church officials——told anxious crowds that they could relieve the pain of their departed loved ones by buying indulgences. "As soon as the coin in the coffer rings," one indulgence hawker said, "the soul from purgatory springs."

The controversy surrounding the sale of indulgences and purgatory proved to be the spark that ignited the Protestant

Reformation when Luther condemned indulgences in his Ninety-five Theses. Criticism of purgatory and indulgences were common themes among the reformers. At his trial for heresy, the Scottish martyr Patrick Hamilton said, "I have never read in the Scripture of such a place as purgatory. The only thing that may purge the souls of men is the blood of Jesus Christ."

CHAPTER 15:
JOHANN OECOLAMPADIUS

The Sweet Fragrance of Christ
(1482–1531)

n 1520, the people of Basel, Switzerland, could hardly believe their ears. "Have you heard," one person told another, "Oecolampadius has become a monk!" Johann Oecolampadius had been the chief preacher in the city's cathedral. People flocked to hear his arresting sermons even though he did not entertain them with jokes as some other preachers did. "What has a preacher of repentance to do with fun and laughter?" he said. "If we can get repentance by laughter, what is the use of repenting in sackcloth and ashes? No one knows that Jesus laughed, but everyone knows that He wept."

Although Oecolampadius took his calling seriously and told the people to trust in God, he did not agree with the German reformer, Martin Luther, who had recently begun exposing errors in the Church of Rome. Oecolampadius accepted the sacrifice of the mass, prayers to Mary and other practices not found in Scripture. Then suddenly, he renounced his calling as a preacher and fled to a monastery in Germany. His friend Erasmus, the famous humanist scholar, was as shocked as everyone else. Oecolampadius had helped Erasmus prepare his Greek New Testament for publication. His mastery of Greek and Hebrew greatly impressed Erasmus who considered him one of Europe's finest linguists. "I hear," Erasmus told a friend, "that Oecolampadius is turned a monk. I wish he had thought it through more carefully."

However, as Oecolampadius prayerfully examined the Scriptures and the writings of Martin Luther in his abbey cell, his thinking changed. He put his trust in Jesus Christ only for the forgiveness of his sins. Then he wrote a booklet confessing his new faith in Christ and opposing unscriptural teachings in the Roman church. He urged his fellow monks to stop relying on the saints or the pope or their own good works. "Look to Christ alone for salvation," he told them. The monks reacted with anger, and they feared that they would be accused of harboring a heretic. Oecolampadius left the monastery in haste. "I lost the monk," he told a friend, "but found the Christian!"

Before long, he accepted a call to St. Martin's Church in Basel——a humble post compared to his former role in the great cathedral. Through his preaching and writing, he proclaimed Christ and called for reforms in the church. Luther read his books with admiration. "May God grant him growth," Luther said.

Sunday by Sunday, large crowds jammed St. Martin's to hear him preach through whole books of the Bible. Many came out to listen to him teach on weekdays too. But Oecolampadius met resistance from the leaders of Basel. Often, he was hauled before the city council to defend his teaching. His explanations won over many councilmen. Over time, the council worked with him to reform the city's churches——allowing services to be conducted in German instead of Latin and removing images and shrines. Oecolampadius sent out traveling preachers to tell poor farmers and shepherds living in remote glens the good news of the grace of God in Jesus' sacrifice for sinners. "It is easy to instill a few doctrines into the ears of our hearers," he told his preachers, "but to change their hearts is in the power of God alone."

When fierce persecution against Evangelicals raged in France, many fled to Switzerland and found a haven in Basel. Oecolampadius helped to organize relief efforts for these poor refugees. One of these was William Farel whom Oecolampadius encouraged to become a minister. Farel went on to be a great evangelist. Exiled preachers smuggled French Bibles and Christian tracts printed in Basel into France.

Several Swiss cities held debates to consider the teachings of the reformers. Oecolampadius often spoke on behalf of the Evangelicals. "We recognize no other rule of judgment than the Word of God," Oecolampadius declared.

"If only this pale man were on our side!" said one supporter of the Roman church. Oecolampadius's piety impressed his adversaries as well. "He must be a holy heretic," a priest said, "because he is always found reading the Scripture or praying."

Emperor Charles V, the most powerful man in Europe, opposed the Reformation. As the king of Spain, emperor of Germany, and ruler over the Netherlands and most of Italy, he could assemble vast armies to do his bidding. In the later 1520s, Charles prepared to crush the Reformation by force. Prince Philip, the Protestant ruler of the German principality of Hesse, believed that the only way to prevent Charles from succeeding was to unify the Protestant cities and provinces in Switzerland and Germany for mutual protection. He worried that the disagreement of the Swiss and German reformers over the Lord's Supper would hinder their stand against Charles and the Roman church. Philip hoped that in a friendly, face-to-face discussion, the key Protestant ministers would find common ground. Since Oecolampadius had written an influential book on the Lord's Supper, Philip invited him along with Zwingli, Bucer, Luther, Melanchthon and others to his castle in Marburg in 1529 for a colloquy to discuss their theological views.

The prince worried that the fiery Luther and the outspoken Zwingli would clash from the start. So, at first, he had Luther meet privately with the tactful Oecolampadius. And he placed Zwingli with the mild-mannered Melanchthon. For several hours, these pairs discussed many of the central teachings of the Christian faith. They agreed on all doctrines except the Lord's Supper. Then all the reformers met in one of the castle's large halls to discuss the meaning of the Lord's Supper.

Prince Philip welcomed the distinguished theologians and encouraged them to discuss their differences and find agreement. As soon as the prince took his seat, Martin Luther stood up and walked to the center of the room to a large wooden table. Pulling a piece of chalk from his pocket, he wrote in bold capital letters on the cloth the Latin words: HOC EST CORPUS MEUM——which means "This is My body."

Luther looked the Swiss reformers in the eyes and said, "I differ from my adversaries in regards to the doctrine of the Supper, and I always will. Christ said, 'This is my body.' Let anyone show me, if he can, that a body is not a body. I reject reason, common sense and the arguments of philosophy. We have the Word of God. We must adore it and obey it."

Then Oecolampadius arose. He agreed that all of Christ's words are true and must be believed. "However," he said, "it cannot be denied that there are figures of speech in the Word of God. Christ called Himself a rock and a vine. Christ's words, 'This is My body,' is a figure of speech of the same kind. Christ was saying that the bread signifies His body, not that it is His physical body."

"Yes, Christ used figurative language at times," Luther admitted. Then he pointed at the chalk letters on the table and said, "But when He said, 'This is My body,' it was not a figure of speech."

"In John chapter 6," Oecolampadius said, "Christ tells the men of Capernaum, 'It is the spirit that gives life, the flesh profits nothing.' In these very words, Christ rejected the idea that in the Supper we are eating His body with the mouth. Since we have a spiritual eating, what need is there of material eating?"

"I do not ask what need there is of it," Luther answered, "but since it is written, 'This is My body,' we must believe it and do it without question."

Oecolampadius kept laboring to find common ground. "Doctor Luther," he said, "let us consider in a friendly way, what is the nature of the presence of Christ's body."

"No," Luther responded, "you will not make me go one step further." Pointing to the words on the table, he said, "Look! This is our passage. You have not got rid of that yet, and we don't care about any other proofs."

"If that is the case," Oecolampadius sighed, "we had better stop disputing."

"Brothers," Prince Philip said, "I implore you to come to some understanding."

"There is but one way to do that," Luther said. "Our opponents must accept our views."

"That we cannot do," replied the Swiss reformers.

"Well then," Luther said, "I abandon you to God's judgment and pray that He will enlighten you."

"We will do the same," Oecolampadius replied.

In the end, the reformers agreed to write up a document that highlighted what they believed in common, but a great opportunity for Protestant unity was lost at the Marburg Colloquy.

Two years later, in the fall of 1531, the Reformation in Switzerland suffered a severe blow, when Zwingli was killed on a battlefield. And then just a few weeks later, Oecolampadius fell sick and died.

Oecolampadius's writings continued to lead people to Jesus Christ long after his death. John Calvin, the greatest of the Reformation theologians, admired his works and was influenced by them. Perhaps Zwingli described Oecolampadius best when he said, "This gentle and steadfast man shed around him the sweet fragrance of Christ."

CHAPTER 16:
WILLIAM FAREL

Elijah of the Swiss Reformation

(1489–1565)

⟜————————⟨

In the summer of 1524, Oecolampadius——the reformer of Basel, Switzerland——ordained William Farel to the Christian ministry, saying, "Now go and feed the flock of God." Farel was a slender, red-bearded Frenchman who had barely escaped France with his life when the king and the bishops unleashed a violent persecution against Evangelicals. When Farel found sanctuary in Switzerland, Oecolampadius befriended him. He saw in the fiery Farel the faith and zeal of a mighty man of God.

Farel's heart ached for his lost countrymen and for the French-speaking Swiss who knew nothing of the full forgiveness of God in Jesus Christ. Like them, Farel had been raised in the teachings of the Church of Rome. As a young adult, he prayed the rosary daily as he prostrated himself before the stations of the cross or adorned with flowers an image of the Virgin Mary. He visited monasteries and aspired to be a monk. When the ideas of the German reformer, Martin Luther, spread into France, Farel gnashed his teeth and staunchly defended the teachings of the Roman church.

But when he was a student at the University of Paris, Farel met a theology professor named Jacques Lefevre. Lefevre's love of the Scriptures inspired Farel to read them for himself, fully expecting that he would find described in its pages the beliefs and the practices of the Roman church. As he read the Scriptures, he saw Jesus Christ and His sacrifice for sin at the center of everything. He did not find prayer to saints or the adoration of Mary or purgatory or papal pardons. "Now," Farel said, "the Scriptures shed great light upon my soul. I hear the voice of Christ my Shepherd, my Master, my Teacher speak to me with power."

He poured himself into learning Greek and Hebrew and gave every spare moment to studying the Bible. Farel began to lead others to the Christ of the Scriptures, and he spoke out against the unbiblical teachings of the church. Church leaders considered him a dangerous heretic. When Farel heard that they plotted to seize him, he fled to Switzerland.

Now——with Oecolampadius's charge ringing in his ears——Farel went out to preach the cross of Jesus Christ, the only hope for sinners. He faced fierce opposition from the start. As he preached in private houses and public squares, he was shouted at, beaten, and run out of one Swiss town after another. Church officials spread the word far and wide, "Don't listen to that devil William Farel!"

Despairing of ever winning a hearing, he tried a different strategy. In the fall of 1526, he came to Aigle, a Swiss alpine town. He called himself Ursinus and said he had come to teach school. Parents could hardly believe their good fortune——it was rare for a university-educated scholar to teach in an out-of-the-way place like Aigle. Soon, Farel was educating a room full of pupils. He not only instructed his students in Latin, mathematics and logic, but he taught them the Scriptures. They learned about Christ and His sacrifice for sinners. The children brought the message back to their families. Before long, the parents came to hear Farel teach about the Savior.

After several months——when Farel thought the time was ripe——he stood up in church when the Sunday service ended and announced, "I am William Farel, minister of God." Then he walked up to the pulpit and began to preach. "Flee your idolatry and look to Jesus Christ alone for grace and forgiveness," he told them. Outraged priests complained to the governor. "It is the devil himself who preaches by the mouth of Farel," they declared. "All those who listen to him will be damned!"

"I charge you to prove the errors that you claim that I am preaching," Farel told his critics, "for I would rather die than teach false doctrine to the poor people whom Christ has redeemed by His blood."

At that time, Aigle was allied with Bern, the powerful Swiss canton which had embraced the Reformation and supported Farel's preaching. "You must allow the very learned William Farel," the Bern council wrote the authorities in Aigle, "to preach publicly the doctrines of the Lord."

Although the leaders of Aigle permitted him to preach, his opponents would gather outside the sanctuary and scream, "Down with Farel!" Once, a gang rushed upon him in church, overturned the pulpit, dragged him outside and beat him. But week by week, more men and women, boys and girls, stopped relying on religious works to win God's favor and put their trust in Christ and walked daily with Him.

After a few more months in Aigle, Farel moved on to bring the light of God's Word to other places. He met stiff resistance wherever he went. Once, when he had tried to preach in a small Swiss town, he and a friend fled for their lives from an angry mob. As they raced down the steep mountain path, a hail of stones hit them from the ridge above. Then a band of priests and townspeople armed with clubs fell upon them. The assailants dragged the half-dead preachers toward a cliff above a roaring river. "Drown them!" they cried.

"No," someone said, "don't kill them yet. Let's lock them up and force them to reveal the names of all those that they have infected with their heresies."

As they hauled the badly wounded men to the castle prison, they passed a statue of the Virgin Mary. "Kneel down before our Lady," they demanded.

Farel shook his head and said, "You ought to worship the only true God and not a dumb and lifeless image." After beating Farel to a pulp, they cast him and his friend into a dungeon cell. But before the local authorities could question and then execute the prisoners, officers from Bern arrived and demanded that the preachers be freed. Fearing the wrath of Bern's council, they released them. Bedridden for three months, Farel slowly recovered from his wounds. "We must endure much reproach," he told another traveling preacher. "We must expect to meet with ingratitude in return for kindness, and evil for good."

Several times, Farel tried to preach in Neuchatel, but each time, the enemies of reform violently expelled him from the city. Again and again, he returned to preach in houses, shops and barns.

Despite the opposition of the priests, many people came to faith in Jesus Christ. A few weeks later, a large crowd brought Farel to the cathedral. "Come to Christ alone for forgiveness," he preached. "The pope's pardons take away money, but they cannot take away sin."

A number of his hearers wept as they considered their sins and idolatry. "We'll follow the Evangelical religion," one man cried out, "both we and our children, and we will live and die in it." Soon, the people stripped the cathedral of its images and insisted on biblical preaching. Many priests looked to Christ for full forgiveness and rejoiced that He freed them forever from the wrath of God. They began to teach the Word of God. "If I have been a good priest," one man told his congregation, "I desire from now on, by God's grace, to be a better pastor."

Farel left Neuchatel, wandering the slopes and valleys of western Switzerland, spreading the word of Christ's love for sinners. As the spiritual awakening grew, Farel's thoughts often turned to the French-speaking, city-state of Geneva. In October 1532, Farel arrived in Geneva with a letter from the Council of Bern, requesting permission to preach in the city. The request was denied. Although they closed the churches to him, he met with small groups who came to his lodgings. Farel opened the Scriptures and brought them the message of Jesus Christ. They carried it back to their homes and neighborhoods, and word of his teaching spread throughout Geneva. The priests, monks and nuns stirred up a crowd who demanded that Farel leave at once or be cast out by force. The Council of Geneva, worried that a riot might break out, brought Farel to a meeting of church officials and magistrates.

"William Farel," said a churchman, "you wicked devil——you're the man that spread heresy in Aigle and Neuchatel. You threw the whole country into confusion!"

"My lords," Farel answered, "I am not a devil. I journey to and fro to preach Jesus Christ. I am compelled to teach Him to all who will hear me. I am ready to prove out of God's Word that my doctrine is true, and I will shed the last drop of my blood for it."

When he tried to explain his teachings from the Scriptures, they shouted him down. "He's guilty of death!" one priest cried. "Kill him! It's better for this rascally Lutheran to die than to let him trouble all the people."

Some magistrates restrained the clergymen from beating him to death on the spot. In the end, the authorities ordered Farel out of the city. As they led him away, a man tried to shoot Farel, but his pistol misfired. Then another assailant rushed at him with a sword, but a magistrate seized the assassin before he reached Farel. He left Geneva, but Farel did not give up hope of winning the city for Christ. He asked his friend, Froment, to go to Geneva and proclaim the gift of eternal life in Jesus. "Alas!" Froment said, "How can I face the enemies from whom you had to flee?"

"Begin, as I began at Aigle," Farel told him. "Go as a schoolmaster and teach the children first." Froment went to Geneva and won many children and then adults to Christ, but after a time, opposition grew, and they expelled him. Farel sent others, but eventually they were thrown out also. Although church leaders in Geneva ordered the destruction of all French Bibles and threatened Evangelicals with banishment, a growing body of believers met in homes or gardens to read the Scriptures and worship God.

Through the urging of Bern, the Council of Geneva permitted a debate on the Evangelical doctrines. Farel spoke for the Evangelicals and a friar defended the teachings of the Church of Rome. Farel won the debate when the friar could not support some of the teachings of the Roman church from Scripture. "Only the welcome doctrine of salvation by Christ can prevent man from utter despair," Farel told them. The council permitted Farel to preach openly in two of the city's churches. The pope demanded that the Genevan councilmen expel the Evangelicals. When they refused, he excommunicated all of the Genevans from the Roman church. The citizens reacted by destroying religious images and demanding the removal of the bishops and priests who would not accept the Evangelical faith. By the summer of 1534, the council forbade the mass and ordered biblical preaching in the churches.

The work of reforming the ministers and people of Geneva was overwhelming. Farel felt unequal to the task, and he called for Evangelical ministers to come to Geneva and assist him. In 1536, he convinced John Calvin, who was passing through Geneva, to stay and help him.

Together, they drafted a confession of faith, revised the worship services, taught the ministers and people and trained missionary preachers to evangelize France and Switzerland. Eventually, the Genevan council resisted the reforms of Farel and Calvin and banished them from the city. After a few years, they brought Calvin back to Geneva, and Farel went to lead the churches in Neuchatel. Geneva became a haven for Protestant refugees from across Europe and a great center for Evangelical teaching. Farel and Calvin remained close friends and partners in the Reformation of Switzerland and France. Calvin called Farel "my best and truest brother." Farel lived to the age of seventy-six, preaching, teaching and praying to the end. Later, he was called "The Elijah of the Swiss Reformation."

CHAPTER 17:
JOHN CALVIN

A Heart Aflame for Christ
(1509–1564)

On November 1, 1533, students and faculty of the Sorbonne, the theological college of the University of Paris, together with a crowd of monks, priests and church officials, filled the college church to hear Professor Nicholas Cop deliver an address. Unbeknownst to most in the audience, Cop had recently embraced the teachings of the Reformation. His Evangelical friend, John Calvin, had written the speech that Cop delivered. "It is only by the grace of God that man can find forgiveness and eternal life in Jesus Christ," he said. As he continued, it didn't take long for the audience to realize that Cop was proclaiming the message of the Protestant reformers—a message that French church leaders and the professors of the Sorbonne fiercely opposed. Recently, the authorities had burned several Frenchmen at the stake for teaching what Cop was preaching from the pulpit. By the time he finished speaking, loud grumbling erupted from the audience. A group of red-faced churchmen immediately denounced Cop to government officials and called for his arrest. Cop got wind of it and fled to Switzerland before he could be tried and executed for his faith.

The next day, John Calvin, unaware that his part in Cop's message had been discovered, sat studying in his college room, when friends burst in, saying, "Your arrest has been ordered. Flee at once!" Moments later, they heard a loud banging at the front gate and shouting from officers of the law demanding entry. Tearing the sheets from his bed, Calvin and his friends tied them together and lowered him to the street below. He raced through back alleys until he reached a friend's home on the edge of the city. Putting on the clothes of a field-hand and carrying a hoe on his shoulder, Calvin escaped into the French countryside.

Not long after, he accepted an invitation from Queen Margaret of Navarre. She used her little kingdom on the southwest border of France as a refuge for persecuted French Evangelicals like Jacques Lefevre. Calvin had long wanted to meet Lefevre whose French translation of the Scriptures had led many to Christ. When eighty-eight-year-old Lefevre and twenty-four-year-old Calvin met in Navarre, they talked for hours. Lefevre encouraged him and predicted that God would do great things through Calvin.

When French authorities pressured Margaret to stop harboring Protestants, Calvin escaped to Basel, Switzerland. There, in March 1536, Calvin published the *Institutes of Christian Religion*——a handbook on Christian theology that showed that Evangelical teaching was true to the Scriptures. Evangelicals in France and Switzerland immediately recognized it as a masterpiece of Christian thought and writing that clearly explained the central teachings of the Word of God. Calvin continued to revise and expand the *Institutes* over the next twenty-five years. It became the most influential book of the Protestant Reformation.

As a wanted fugitive condemned by the Church of Rome and king of France, Calvin kept on the move to avoid arrest. He used a false name and slipped in and out of France to preach in secret to small groups of Evangelicals. In July 1536, Calvin's escape route led him through Geneva. He registered at an inn under the name Charles d'Espeville, went straight to his room, grateful for a chance to read and rest. But this was not to be; for as he entered the city, he had been seen and recognized. As he settled in for the night, he heard a knock at his door. "Who's there?" he asked.

"William Farel," a strong voice answered. Farel, widely known as a bold preacher, was leading Geneva away from the traditions of the Church of Rome and back to the teachings of the Scriptures. Calvin invited him in. Although Farel's body was short and weak, he burst into the room like a thunderstorm. His sunburned face and red hair matched his fiery personality. "Mr. Calvin," he said, pumping Calvin's hand vigorously, "thank God you're here. You must join me in the work at once!"

"I don't understand, sir," Calvin said, "I will be leaving Geneva in the morning."

"No," Farel replied, "I'm afraid that won't do. We must have you here. The reformation of this city has just begun and I need your help."

"But sir," Calvin said, "I'm a scholar, and I'm too timid and inexperienced for such a work. I plan to devote my energies to private study and writing." Unwilling to take no for an answer, Farel pled with Calvin to stay and teach the people and organize the church.

Calvin remained unmoved. "Mr. Farel," he said, "my plans are set. I must keep free from other duties to study and write."

Farel leaned forward in his chair, his eyes ablaze. Pointing his finger at Calvin he warned in a loud voice, "You are following your own wishes, and I tell you in the name of God Almighty, that if you do not help us in this work of the Lord, the Lord will punish you for seeking your own interests rather than His."

Calvin sat trembling in shocked silence, terror-struck. Farel's words came to him as if from an Old Testament prophet. "I felt," he later said, "as if God from on high had stretched out His hand and took hold of me." He agreed to stay in Geneva.

Shortly after Calvin arrived in Geneva, the city leaders of Lausanne held a religious debate. The citizens crowded into the cathedral to hear an open discussion between the Evangelicals and the Roman Catholics. One hundred seventy-four Roman clergymen attended. Farel, the chief spokesman for the Evangelicals, brought Calvin along. For three days they debated, but Calvin said nothing.

Farel prodded him to speak but Calvin said, "You are answering the questions well. Why should I interfere?"

"But you have so much insight and knowledge," Farel said. "It's a shame your shyness keeps you from using it."

On the fourth day, a priest claimed the writings of Augustine and the early church fathers supported the teachings of the Church of Rome. "You men," he said, pointing his finger at the reformers, "stand against the church fathers." Farel, uncertain how to answer, prepared to stammer a reply when suddenly Calvin rose to speak. All eyes were fixed upon him.

"Honor to the holy church fathers," he said, looking the priest squarely in the eyes. "If you read them more carefully, you would not speak as you do." For over an hour he quoted from memory whole passages from Augustine, Tertullian and others, arguing that the church fathers agreed with Scripture and the Evangelicals. "Judge for yourselves whether we are hostile to the church fathers," he said, "and admit that you hardly know what they taught." When Calvin finished, he had destroyed the arguments of the priests. Not a single man stood up to refute him. No one in the audience had ever heard anything like it.

After several minutes of awkward silence, a Franciscan friar, his gray robe tied about his waist with a rope, stepped forward. He was John Tandy, a preacher and sworn enemy of the Protestants. "Based on what I have just heard," he said, "I confess that I have sinned against the Spirit and rebelled against the truth. Because of ignorance, I have lived in error and spread wrong teaching. I ask God's pardon and the forgiveness of the people of Lausanne. I give up my role as friar; from now on I will follow Christ and His pure teaching alone." Not long after the debate, more than one hundred priests, monks and friars became Evangelicals. Lausanne was won for the Reformation.

The council in Geneva appointed Calvin to teach theology and preach. Every day he taught classes on the Scriptures and Christian doctrine to ministers and parishioners alike. His theological teaching was desperately needed as most of the ministers of the city were unable to explain or defend Evangelical teaching. After his first sermon, a large crowd followed him to his house, imploring him to preach again the next day. Calvin preached several times a week, pointing the people to Christ. "God has shown His mercy to poor sinners on the way to ruin," he preached. "Jesus Christ appeared for the salvation of the world. Believe in Him——the gate of paradise is opened to us, purchased for us by our Lord Jesus Christ. He is ready to receive us."

His preaching challenged the people of Geneva——a city famous for its immorality——to live holy lives. "If we desire salvation," he said, "we must receive His Word with obedience and faith." Many people embraced Jesus Christ for the forgiveness of their sins and, by the grace of God, strove to walk faithfully with Him. But others resented Calvin's forthright call to repent and obey the commandments of God. They wanted to live as they pleased. His enemies pressured the city council to get rid of Calvin and Farel. In 1538, the council summoned the two ministers and declared, "We hereby banish you from Geneva. You have three days to depart."

"Very well," the reformers replied, "it is better to serve God than man."

The expulsion proved to be a great blessing for Calvin. He went to Strasbourg at the invitation of the Evangelical leader, Martin Bucer, who took him into his home for a time and set Calvin up as the minister to a group of French Protestant refugees. From Bucer, Calvin learned a great deal about pastoring a flock, leading worship and organizing a congregation. In Strasbourg, Calvin married Idelette de Bure, a Christian widow with two children. He wrote a commentary on Romans and helped to a write a French Psalm book for congregational singing.

While Calvin thrived in Strasbourg and enjoyed the happiest years of his life, things went from bad to worse in Geneva. Crude sin abounded. Strife and troubles divided the city into factions, leading to frequent brawls and even murder. A growing number of citizens called for Calvin's return. In spring 1541, the Genevan council voted unanimously to bring Calvin back. But he did not want to go. "Who will blame me," he told a friend, "if I do not willingly throw myself again into a whirlpool that I found so fatal? I can scarcely believe that my ministry will be of any use to them."

Through the urging of Farel and Bucer, Calvin agreed to return. With his wife and children, he moved into a house near St. Peter's Cathedral. He threw himself into the work, sleeping just four hours each night. Every day he preached and gave lectures on the Scriptures. Calvin emphasized God's sovereignty over all things and His love and mercy for His children. "Christ came," he preached, "to swallow up death and replace it with life——to conquer sin and replace it with righteousness."

Shunning the hierarchical system of government of the Church of Rome with its pope and bishops, he implemented a presbyterian form of church rule where ministers and ruling elders chosen from the congregation led the church. Godly men were chosen as deacons to care for the poor and the sick.

In addition to preaching, teaching and counseling, Calvin started a college and wrote commentaries on most of the books of the Bible. He taught the people that God called them to love others and to use their resources to help the needy. "All the blessings we enjoy are divine gifts," he preached, "committed to our trust on this condition, that they should be used for the benefit of our neighbors."

Over time, Geneva was transformed. Brawling and drunkenness greatly diminished. It was said that prayer and psalm singing never ceased in the city. They built a hospital, schools and homes for the poor and cared for widows and orphans. As persecution against Evangelicals heated up across Europe, thousands of refugees fled to Geneva for safety, and the Genevan church generously provided for their needs. Protestants from France, England, Scotland, Holland, Spain, Italy and other lands not only found protection, but they also learned from Calvin and followed the example of the Genevan church. When the Scotsman John Knox arrived in Geneva, he marveled at the church and its ways. "It is the most perfect school of Christ on earth since the days of the apostles," he said. When he returned to Scotland and led the Reformation there, Knox modeled the Church of Scotland after Calvin's Geneva. English, Dutch and French refugees did the same in their lands. Fifty years after the death of Calvin, English Puritans brought the Evangelical faith——shaped by Calvin's teaching on the Scriptures——to New England. And later, missionaries spread it throughout the world.

Calvin took as his life's motto: "My heart aflame I give you, Lord, promptly and sincerely." He had an artist depict the motto in an emblem showing a flaming heart in the palm of a hand. Through many decades of service, he strove, by God's grace, to put his motto into practice. Nearly five hundred years later, John Calvin's writings continue to point sinners to Jesus Christ and instruct Christians in the deepest truths of the Bible.

CHAPTER 18:
GASPARD DE COLIGNY

Defender of the Huguenots
(1519–1572)

In 1559, French Protestants, the Huguenots, had had enough. Despite their loyalty to the crown and their faithful service to France in her wars against Spain, they had endured decades of persecution from the government. Though burned at the stake, drowned in rivers and cut down by the sword, the number of Huguenots grew. When young King Francis II had ascended the throne a few months earlier, they had hoped for better things. But Francis was dominated by his mother and the Guise family—all staunch Roman Catholics who viewed the Huguenots as dangerous heretics. They convinced Francis to launch an attack against the Huguenots. Officials plastered crude posters in Paris and other cities depicting Protestants torturing priests, stomping on the Eucharist and defacing religious statues.

Throughout the kingdom, soldiers burst into Huguenot homes, murdering fathers and mothers, stealing their property and casting their children out into the cold. Protestant nobles who came to the royal court to protest the violence were thrown out. The highest ranking Huguenot, Prince Louis de Condé, called a meeting of Protestant nobles. "Let us fly to arms!" Condé demanded. Others agreed that the Huguenots must form an army and fight back. But then Admiral Gaspard de Coligny stood up. The grave Coligny was held in high esteem by all of France. His godly character and calm demeanor under pressure won him high office in the kingdom. He counseled patience. "Is it necessary to take up arms," he asked the other Huguenot nobles, "in order to put an end to this grisly persecution of the church of Christ which dishonors and compromises the kingdom? The king is young; let us appeal to him and the queen mother for redress." He reminded the men that a civil war would wreak havoc on the land and lead to the death of thousands of innocents. Coligny convinced the Huguenot leaders that they were not yet strong enough to fight a civil war and that they needed first to cultivate the help of the Protestants in Germany and England.

When Francis died suddenly during his first year on the throne, the queen mother, Catherine de Medici, served as regent for her younger son Charles who was crowned king to replace his deceased brother. Coligny petitioned the boy king and his mother on behalf of the Huguenots. "The gospel which we profess teaches us our duty toward your majesty," he told them. "We understand more clearly our submission to the governing authorities by means of the holy doctrine that is preached to us."

Seeking to avoid a clash between the Roman Catholics and the Huguenots, Catherine tried to end the persecution by issuing the

Edict of January in 1562. For the first time, it granted Protestants legal standing in France and permitted the Huguenots to hold public worship services outside of towns. Clergy of the Church of Rome and Roman Catholic noblemen loudly protested against any compromise with the Huguenots.

Then one Sunday morning in February 1562, several hundred Huguenots gathered for worship in a barn outside the town of Vassy. It happened that the duke of Guise and a company of his soldiers were riding on the road near Vassy when they heard the Huguenots worshiping. The duke and his men burst into the barn and opened fire on the unarmed congregants, killing more than sixty men, women and children and wounding two hundred others.

When word reached Condé, he called on all French Protestants to take up arms. Although outraged at the massacre, Coligny hesitated to call for war, knowing the devastation it would rain down on the kingdom. But soon news came that royal troops were massacring Huguenots in towns and cities across France. So Coligny set out at once to join Condé, gathering men as he went.

Coligny, the most experienced military man of the Huguenots, insisted on discipline within the Huguenot forces. He called for morning and evening prayers to be said in each regiment, encouraging the men to pray for the king and to ask God's help to guard their behavior. Wherever the Huguenot army went, Coligny let it be known that they were not fighting against the king, but against the Guises who violated the law of the land by attacking Huguenots. Marauding Roman Catholic troops slaughtered thousands of Protestant civilians. Huguenot refugees fled for safety to the towns held by Coligny's forces. But discipline proved nearly impossible to maintain in the Huguenot ranks. Despite Coligny's best efforts, Huguenot troops, enraged by the massacres of their brothers and sisters, killed Roman Catholic priests and destroyed Catholic churches and shrines.

In the midst of the war, Coligny heard that his home had been ransacked by the enemy and all his valuables stolen. "We must not count upon property," he wrote to his sons, "but rather place our hope elsewhere than on earth… Men have taken from us all they can. If such is the will of God, we shall be happy."

The war did not go well for the Huguenots as help from Germany and England was meager and the Roman Catholic forces greatly outnumbered them in men and artillery. At one point, a Huguenot spy stole into the Guise camp and assassinated Francis, the duke of Guise. Although Coligny had nothing to do with the murder, the Guise family blamed him for it.

After a year of fighting, Condé was taken prisoner and a short time later——without consulting Coligny——he signed a peace treaty to end the civil war. The treaty was a disaster for the Protestants, stripping them of some of the liberties granted to them by the Edict of January. The treaty allowed Huguenot nobles to practice their faith in their own homes, but it forbade Protestant worship in Paris. It set aside the outskirts of a few towns in each county where the Huguenots could hold worship services——often long distances from Huguenot homes. Coligny believed the treaty placed undue hardships on the Huguenots. "What about the poor who fought as bravely as the nobles?" he complained to Condé. "They must walk many miles——women, children, the feeble and the aged——or have no public worship at all."

But the deed was done and Coligny disbanded his forces and returned peacefully to his estate. The Guises pressed the queen mother to bring Coligny to trial for conspiring to murder Francis Guise. Eventually, the crown exonerated Coligny from any wrongdoing in the matter, but the Guise family thirsted for revenge.

Every morning Coligny rose early for private prayer. Then he prayed with his family and the servants of the household. He read the Scriptures aloud, and then they heard a sermon from a minister and sang a psalm. In the evening, he prayed with his family and household again and closed the day by singing a psalm of thanksgiving. He took care to teach his children the Scriptures and catechize them in the Reformed faith. Coligny followed the same pattern when he was at war in his military camp. His devotional life set an example for the French nobility and his soldiers to follow. Coligny greatly appreciated Calvin's sermons on Job and often read one of them each day. "This story," he said of Job, "is the consolation of my soul and God's sovereign remedy in my distress."

In the coming seven years, two more civil wars of religion were fought as the Huguenots struggled for survival. Because Coligny was the glue that held the Huguenots and their army together, the French parliament put a price on his head of 50,000 crowns. Before long, both Prince Condé and Andelot——Coligny's brother and a key Huguenot general——were killed in the fighting. Coligny's closest allies were Jeanne d' Albret,* queen of Navarre, and her son Henry, an heir to the throne of France. Coligny discipled Henry in the art of war, and Henry became an important Huguenot officer.

However, after several defeats the Huguenot cause appeared lost. Then through a desperate but brilliant military campaign, Coligny forced the enemy to come to terms. Both sides, exhausted and decimated from the war, signed a peace treaty that granted Protestants the right to hold public worship services in every town. In order to strengthen the peace, the queen mother suggested that the leading

---

* Read about Jeanne d' Albret in *Radiant: Fifty Remarkable Women in Church History* (2015).

Huguenot prince, Henry of Navarre, marry her daughter Margaret, hoping that if a Huguenot prince married a Catholic princess that peace would be secured.

Gaspard Coligny returned to his castle at Chatillion in central France determined to make religious tolerance a reality in the kingdom where Catholics and Protestants could live side-by-side in peace. In the district that he controlled——that was majority Huguenot——he restored some churches to Roman Catholic worship and saw to it that Catholic priests and worshipers were not harassed. It was said that there was no place in France where priests could live in greater safety then in Chatillion.

Coligny took steps to assure young King Charles and his mother Catherine of his loyalty and the loyalty of the Huguenots. At great risk to himself, he left his castle and served at the court in Paris alongside his enemies, the Guises. King Charles IX admired Coligny's military prowess and grew to appreciate his integrity and candor. Coligny urged the king to send a French army of Huguenots and Catholics to fight with the Protestants of the Netherlands in their effort to win independence from France's long-time enemy, Spain. Catherine resented Coligny's growing influence over her son, so she secretly conspired with the Guises to murder him.

On August 18, 1572, Henry of Navarre married Princess Margaret in Paris. Huguenot leaders from all France gathered for the royal wedding. But Catherine and the Guises hired an assassin to kill Gaspard de Coligny. A few days after the wedding, a gunman shot Coligny as he walked outside his Paris hotel. The bullet ripped through a finger and shattered his left elbow. Friends carried the bleeding Coligny to his room, crying for their wounded leader. "My friends," he said, "why do you weep for me? I am happy to receive these wounds for the cause of God."

Angry Huguenots took to the streets and demanded justice, blaming the Guise family for the crime. Catherine and the duke of Guise, fearing that Huguenots would retaliate for the attempt on Coligny's life, decided to slaughter the Huguenots in Paris. Catherine and Guise went to the king and told him that the Huguenots planned to start another civil war. They warned Charles that the Huguenots must be wiped out or he would never control France. Charles's cheeks flushed red as he shouted, "By God's death! I want all the Huguenots of France killed!"

The duke of Guise sprang into action, leading three hundred soldiers to the gate of Coligny's lodgings. They slew the guard and rushed in. Coligny's friends barricaded the hallway. One man ran into Coligny's room and said, "They have broken in and we cannot resist them."

"I have been prepared to die for a long time," Coligny replied. "Save your lives. I commend my soul to the mercy of God."

Moments later, Guise's henchmen burst into the room and found Coligny standing up, leaning against the wall. The intruders quickly dispatched him with battle ax and sword.

As the sun rose, archers, horsemen and foot soldiers fanned out across Paris to attack the 10,000 Huguenots visiting the city. The Paris rabble joined in when the king's soldiers shouted: "Kill them! Massacre the Huguenots!"

Mobs ran wild through the streets, breaking into houses, killing Huguenots—running them through with daggers or throwing them headlong from buildings. They knocked little children and old people senseless and cast them into the river to drown. This happened on August 23, 1572, the Feast of St. Bartholomew, so the terrible day is remembered as the St. Bartholomew's Day Massacre. The killing of Huguenots continued across France for weeks. Tens of thousands of men, women and children were slaughtered. Henry of Navarre was held under house arrest in Paris, but after several months, he managed to escape.

The massacre sparked a renewal of war with Henry of Navarre leading the Huguenot cause. Battles raged for many years until Henry was crowned King of France. Although Henry did not hold to the Protestant faith when he became king, he cherished the memory of Gaspard de Coligny all his days. Henry granted religious freedom to both Roman Catholics and Huguenots throughout the land by issuing the Edict of Nantes. And Henry saw to it that the religious liberty that Coligny fought for became a reality in France. Coligny's daughter, Louise, married William the Silent, Prince of Orange, the great defender of the Dutch Protestants. Their descendants were the kings and queens of the Netherlands for centuries. Under their leadership, the Netherlands became a haven for persecuted Christians.

CHAPTER 19:
RENÉE, DUCHESS
OF FERRARA

Protector of the Persecuted

(1510–1575)

In autumn of 1534, King Francis I of France ordered a crackdown on French Protestants, the Huguenots. Agents of the king arrested and tortured Huguenot ministers, and church courts declared them heretics. Francis ordered them burned at the stake as a grand show.

On January 21, 1535, Francis I, wearing robes of purple velvet, and his wife, Queen Claudia, glittering with precious jewels, led a great procession on horseback through Paris. The royalty of France and other dignitaries followed on foot, carrying lighted candles. The churchmen held aloft sacred relics, including items claimed to be

Christ's crown of thorns and Moses' stone tablets of the Ten Commandments. After the procession, they feasted at a lavish banquet and then watched the burning of six Huguenots.

Huguenot leaders fled the country to Germany, Switzerland, Navarre and Ferrara——a small duchy in northern Italy. They escaped to Ferrara for the shelter and hospitality of Renée, duchess of Ferrara. Renée's deceased father was King Louis XII of France, and her sister Claudia reigned as queen of France. Renée's marriage in 1528 to Ercole Este, Duke of Ferrara, was not a marriage of love, but a political arrangement. The tiny duchy of Ferrara, in order to preserve its independence, needed to maintain friendly relations with France, the German empire and the pope. King Francis I, eager to strengthen France's hand in northern Italy, arranged for his sister-in-law, Renée, to marry the duke of Ferrara. But strong religious differences separated the duke and Renée.

Duke Ercole defended the teaching of the Roman church. Renée followed the Protestant reformers and supported Huguenot preachers. Renée's parents died when she was a little girl and she was raised by a governess, Madame de Soubise, who came to her from England with a hidden copy of Wyclif's Bible in her luggage. She opened Renée's eyes to the Word of God. As a teenager, Renée devoured all the writings of the French reformers and later brought Madame de Soubise to Ferrara as a member of her royal court. They prayed, worshiped and studied the Scriptures together and listened to Protestant preachers that Renée brought to her court.

As the persecution in France grew, many Huguenots fled to Renée's court in Ferrara, and among them were Clemont Marot, preacher and translator of the Psalms into French verse, and John Calvin, author of the *Institutes of the Christian Religion*. Renée's activities infuriated her husband. He threw Madame de Soubise out of the royal court and forbade Renée to travel outside of Ferrara. He intercepted her mail and removed Protestants from her court.

After church leaders ordered the arrest of Calvin and Marot, Renée aided their escape. When the pope summoned the Italian preacher, Orchino, to appear before the Inquisition in Rome, Renée helped him to flee from Italy to Geneva, where he worked with Calvin. Renée regularly sent money to the Protestant refugees in Geneva. She brought an Italian scholar, Antonio Bruccioli, to her court and supported his work translating the Bible into Italian.

Priests in Ferrara sent word to the pope, reporting that the duchess ate meat during Lent, refused to attend mass and erected a private chapel in the castle without a crucifix or images of the saints. The pope sent a representative to interrogate Renée. She refused to see him. "My confidence is in God and none other," she told her husband. The duke brought the Inquisition to Ferrara and threw many of his Protestant subjects in jail. Renée asked him to release them. "I beg you very humbly," she wrote him, "to free the prisoners you have sent to the inquisitors. Remember the grief of the poor fathers, mothers and little children of those you have imprisoned." The duke ignored her requests.

When the popular preacher, Fanino Fanini, fell into the duke's hands, Renée pleaded with tears for his release. Fanini preached using Bruccioli's Italian translation of the Bible. When he traveled through Ferrara, Duke Ercole's men seized him and cast him into prison. Many people gathered outside the barred window of his cell to hear Fanini preach the Word of God. To break up the crowds, jailers moved him to an inner cell. Renée had food and fresh clothing sent to him. She fired off letters to church leaders and the king of France on his behalf. The pope demanded that Duke Ercole burn Fanini at once and purge his duchy of all Evangelicals. He complained of Renée's interference on Fanini's behalf. "My wife often acts without our knowledge and against our will," the duke wrote the pope. "As a Christian and Catholic prince, I intend to give Fanini the punishment he deserves."

Under orders from the duke, guards dragged Fanini from his cell, hanged him and burned his body. Then Duke Ercole launched an all-out effort to rid his wife of her heresy, enlisting the help of the king of France. The French king sent several inquisitors at once to Ferrara. For three months, they daily preached to Renée and grilled her on her beliefs and actions on behalf of the Protestants. Renée told them that she was neither a Lutheran nor a Calvinist but simply a Christian. Her defiance forced the duke's hand. He shut up Renée in solitary confinement in the castle and placed a guard outside her door. Her daughters were forbidden to see her and were sent to a convent. The inquisitor threatened her with life imprisonment and even death if she did not recant.

Finally, exhausted and in tears, Renée agreed to confess her sins to a priest and attend mass. Her trial ended, and the duke restored some of her privileges, but he burned all her books and surrounded her with spies. He told her that he did not believe the sincerity of her confession but pretended publicly to believe her to spare the duchy the scandal of heresy. Her son, Alphonso, said that he believed his mother deserved to be burned at the stake as a heretic. For the last five years of their marriage, Renée and the duke remained unreconciled until his death in 1559.

Outwardly Renée conformed, but secretly she kept up her correspondence with Evangelical leaders and sent money to aid Protestant exiles in France and Switzerland. At the death of his father, Alphonso became duke. He detested Protestants more than his father had. "I would rather live with the plague," he said while visiting the French court, "than live with Huguenots."

Shortly after being crowned, he issued an ultimatum to his mother——either she give up her Evangelical faith completely or be banished from Ferrara forever. Rather than abandon her faith, Renée left the country where she had reigned as duchess for thirty-two years and returned to France. "My Son," she wrote in a note as she departed, "I could not say to you what was in my heart for fear of being overwhelmed with tears."

Renée found France on the brink of civil war. The Parliament of Paris declared the death penalty for anyone worshiping as a Protestant. Soldiers and mobs massacred Huguenots in twenty French cities. Enraged Huguenots took up arms, broke into churches, smashed images and shattered windows. In some places, monks and priests were killed. In one city, two hundred people died when a Huguenot mob sacked the cathedral. Renée spoke out against violence. "We are to render good for evil," she urged the Huguenots. "Hate and Christianity are incompatible. We must seek peace with all."

Upon returning to France, Renée took possession of her inheritance, the castle of Montargis. As troubles escalated, she expanded the moat, reinforced the walls, installed cannons and welcomed hundreds of Roman Catholic and Huguenot refugees fleeing the bloodshed. She set up a chapel in the castle for Protestant worship and encouraged the preaching of the good news of Jesus throughout the city. Renée forbade violence from either side and sent her soldiers to stop pillaging and murder whether committed by Roman Catholics or Huguenots.

Battles raged across France, and Roman Catholic forces invaded Montargis. A commander ordered her to surrender her castle, and when she refused he set up cannon and threatened to open fire. Renée told the commander, "Consider well what you are planning to do. There is no one in this kingdom who commands me except the king himself. If you come, I will throw myself into the breach and see whether you will have the audacity to kill the daughter of a king."

The commander backed down and withdrew his forces from the city. The castle and the refugees were saved. Renée's protection and hospitality became known throughout France. Huguenots called her castle "The Hotel of the Lord."

John Calvin rejoiced in her work and wrote, "I know that you have been like a nursing mother to those poor, persecuted brothers and sisters who did not know where to go. God has done you a great honor in allowing you to carry His banner."

While Renée was in Paris in 1572, the king ordered the massacre of Huguenots on St. Bartholomew's Day. Blood ran in the streets, and thousands were slaughtered. Renée could hear their shouts and screams. For a week, she and her ladies remained behind a locked door and an armed guard. She hastily returned to Montargis and threw open the gates of her castle to hundreds of Huguenots fleeing for their lives.

For the next two years, she endured sickness and pain and did what she could to preserve life. She died among her Christian friends but was separated from her children, who rejected her religious beliefs. The king of France forbade her body to be laid to rest in St. Denis, the burial site for French kings and queens and their children. Renée's body was placed in a simple wooden casket and buried without ceremony within her castle walls.

In her will, she left a long statement of her faith in Jesus Christ and concluded with a note to her children: "I pray that my children will read and listen to the Word of God in which they will find comfort and the true guide to eternal life."

"Renée, Duchess of Ferrara: Protector of the Persecuted" is excerpted from *Trial and Triumph: Stories from Church History* (1999).

REFORMATION BASICS 5

The Pope and Papal Bulls

In the early years of Christianity, the church in a particular
locality was ruled by a body of elders. Over time, bishops
emerged as leading churchmen in important cities. During
the Middle Ages, the Church of Rome began to assert that
the bishop of Rome was the direct successor to the Apostle
Peter. It was claimed that Christ had made Peter the rock
upon whom he would build his church and invested him
with special authority as the head of the church and that Peter had served as the first bishop of Rome. Therefore, it was
said that Peter's spiritual authority had been passed down to
each succeeding bishop of Rome. Through the centuries, the
bishop of Rome, who came to be called the pope, controlled
vast tracts of land and wealth and often acted more like a
corrupt worldly prince than a minister of God. The most
important decisions of the pope were written on official
documents that carried the pope's seal. These documents
were called papal bulls.

Protestants accepted the Scriptures alone as the supreme
authority for Christian doctrine and life. They rejected the
pope as the head of the church and refused to accept papal
pronouncements that were contrary to the Scriptures. In
1520, when Pope Leo issued a papal bull declaring Luther a
heretic and condemning all his writings, Luther threw a copy of
the bull into a bonfire saying, "This bull condemns me without
any proof from Scripture. If I am a heretic, then show me from
God's Word."

When the pope condemned the gospel message that sinners are saved by the grace of God through faith in Christ alone and persecuted those who proclaimed it, the reformers concluded that the pope was an enemy of biblical Christianity. Once, when William Tyndale was citing passages from Scripture that showed that forgiveness comes only through faith in Christ, not through papal pardons, a priest shouted, "We would be better off without God's law than the pope's!"

"I defy the pope and all his laws," Tyndale said. "If God spares my life, in a few years a ploughboy shall know more of the Scriptures than you do."

CHAPTER 20:
FANINO FANINI

Italian Reformation Martyr
(1520-1550)

W hen Reformation teaching began to circulate in Italy, the Church of Rome did not respond to it with reasoned debate but with terror. The Scriptures in Italian and the writings of reformers like Luther, Zwingli and Bucer were banned and burned. The pope unleashed spies and inquisitors who prowled the land seeking Evangelicals to devour. Prisons filled with men and women, the high-born and the low. Those who held fast to their faith were left to rot in dungeons or enslaved or slain. "At Rome," one observer said, "some are burned, hanged or beheaded every day. All the prisons are filled, and the city cannot supply enough jails for the number of pious people who are continually apprehended."

Italian reformers were killed, cowered or forced to flee to Germany or Switzerland. Some found refuge for a time in the Italian principality of Ferrara under the protection of Duchess Renée. But even she lived under intense pressure from the pope and her husband, the duke.

The fierce persecution struck terror in the hearts of anyone who contemplated following the Evangelical faith and drove many Protestants to abandon Christ. But here and there, a few Italians found new life in Jesus Christ and held fast to Him.

Now there lived in Faenza, Italy, a baker named Fanino Fanini who bought a contraband copy of the Scriptures in Italian. As he read, the true Christ came to life for him in the straightforward gospel accounts. In his mind's eye, he saw Jesus healing the sick, multiplying the loaves and fishes, and raising the dead. Through it all, he heard Christ calling, "Come unto me all you who are weary and heavy laden and I will give you rest." In the Scriptures he found a large-hearted Savior, a friend of sinners, not the stern and unapproachable Redeemer that Fanini had learned about from the Roman priests. Soon he stopped relying on his own good works or the merits of the saints and put all his trust in Christ.

Fanini memorized many passages of the Old and New Testaments and loved to recite them to his wife and friends. He could not keep the good news to himself but freely shared it with family members and neighbors. Fanini walked to nearby towns to tell those who would listen about Christ's great love for sinners. When agents of the Inquisition discovered his activities, they cast him into prison and threatened him with death, if he refused to recant.

Although harangued and tortured, Fanini would not deny his Savior. "I am ready to be bound, imprisoned and die for the name of Christ," he said. His wife came and implored him to recant to save his life. After repeated pleadings, he succumbed. He renounced his faith and submitted again to the teachings of the Roman church.

As soon as Fanini was released, his joy in Christ vanished, replaced by a grieving conscience. These words of Christ haunted him, "Whoever denies Me before men, I also will deny before My Father who is in heaven." Sorrow and regret weighed him down like iron chains. But after a time of deep despair, Fanini sought God for forgiveness and resolved to proclaim the truth that he had denied. He traveled throughout northern Italy in 1547, discreetly telling a few people at a time about Jesus Christ. Those who believed in Christ, he left to instruct others, and he went to spread the good news elsewhere. Before long, church authorities found him out and arrested him for a second time. They brought him in chains to Ferrara. Fanini had no regrets. "Now I know I have brought forth some fruit to the glory of God," he said.

Inquisitors threatened to stretch him on the rack and burn him at the stake, but he remained unmovable. Then his wife and sister visited his cell. With weeping, they begged him to recant. He refused. "If you do not care for yourself," his wife said, "think of me and our children."

"My Lord does not want me to deny Him for the sake of my family," he told her. "For your sake, I once denied my Savior. Had I known then what I have learned by my fall through the grace of God, I would not have yielded to your wishes. Go home in peace, for my end is near."

However, Fanini remained in prison for two years. Duchess Renée of Ferrara pleaded with her husband to release him, but he would not. Renée visited Fanini in prison, but when the duke restricted her to the palace, she sent Princess Lavinia, an Evangelical friend from a powerful Italian family, to visit him and pray with him.

Many people gathered outside the barred window of Fanini's cell to hear him preach the Word of God. To break up the crowds, jailers moved him to an inner cell. He shared his faith with everyone——prisoners, jailers and visitors. Fanini's winsome character and biblical teaching led many to Christ. In an effort to curtail his influence, the authorities forbade him visitors. When they discovered that many prisoners embraced Fanini's faith, they locked him up in solitary confinement. "I had not known what freedom and happiness were," a released prisoner said, "until through Fanini I found it within the walls of the prison."

His effect was so great on the jailers that church officials ordered the warden to change his guards often.

In the quiet of his cell, Fanini sent letters to friends and wrote out his beliefs, quoting many passages of Scripture from memory in defense of the Evangelical faith. At the top of all his writings he put his motto: "I shall not die but live, and declare the works of the Lord."

In 1550, the newly-elected Pope Julius III commanded that Fanini be put to death at once. Guards moved him to a different jail to await execution where he met new prisoners to lead to Jesus Christ. Princess Lavinia went to Rome and petitioned Pope Julius to spare Fanini's life. With a growl, the pope warned her that it was not safe for her to support a heretic, and he hinted that if she persisted, she might share his fate.

One evening, a messenger came and told Fanini that he would be killed before morning. Fanini hugged him and said, "My dear brother, for the sake of Christ, I accept death joyfully."

Then he told his cellmates, "I am happy to face this death because by it I will enter the eternal happiness of heaven." As Fanini explained to them how they could find everlasting life in Christ, one man interrupted and said, "But what about your children? Who have you assigned to be their guardian?"

"I have left them in the hands of the best of guardians who will carefully protect them," Fanini answered.

"And who is he?" asked the prisoner.

"Our Lord Jesus Christ," Fanini replied.

Just then, guards burst into the cell, clapped his feet in irons and dragged him to a room full of jail officers and the executioner. Fanini quoted Scripture to them and urged them to turn to Christ. One by one, he looked each man in the eye and said, "May God save you, my brother! Rejoice with me because I'm going to heaven."

With a beaming face, Fanini praised God for His glory and mercy. Tears came to the eyes of many of the officers——even the executioner. Then a papal representative arrived and said, "If you recant, the pope will spare your life."

Fanini smiled and told him, "Truth cannot be killed. I have no desire to escape death."

When they brought him back to his cell, Fanini told his fellow captives stories from the life of Christ. Then he recited some Christian poems that he had written on justification by faith and the sovereignty of God and other scriptural themes. One of the prisoners, surprised at the joyful look on Fanini's face, asked him, "How is it that you are so cheerful when Christ suffered such agony before His death?"

"Although Christ had never sinned," Fanini answered, "to satisfy the justice of God He took our sins upon Himself and bore our punishment. Thus when He was in the garden and on the cross He suffered all the pains and tortures of hell which we deserved. This caused His sadness before His death. But I rejoice, since through faith I enjoy the blessings which Christ has purchased for us by His death. I am certain that at the death of my body I shall pass into eternal life. I cannot help but be glad and exult with joy!"

A few hours later, guards led Fanini by torch light through the darkness to a scaffold erected in the center of Ferrara. Church authorities ordered that his execution take place long before sunrise so that no one could hear him speak at the end. When a priest of the Church of Rome held a crucifix in front of his face, Fanini said, "Please do not try to remind me of Christ by a bit of wood, for I hold Him with a lively faith in my heart." Then he knelt and prayed, asking God to open the eyes of the Italian people to see Christ. After the hangman did his work, soldiers burned his body and threw his ashes into the River Po. Later that day, many people of Ferrara gathered around the scaffold and said, "We cannot believe that such a good man deserved to die."

Fanino Fanini's prison writings were secretly copied and circulated among some brave folks who risked the wrath of the inquisitors to read Protestant works. Sadly, the lack of support for the Reformation among any of the Italian princes, and the severe persecution of the Inquisition stamped out all but a tiny remnant of Evangelicals in Italy.

COMPREHENSION QUESTIONS

for Part Three

1. What great gift did Jacques Lefevre give the people of France?

2. How did Ulrich Zwingli come to a living faith in Christ?

3. Why is Zwingli called the "Father of the Swiss Reformation?"

4. How did Oecolampadius advance the French Reformation from Basel?

5. Describe the opposition that William Farel faced as he tried to preach the gospel?

6. How did John Calvin end up being a minister in Geneva?

7. In what significant ways did John Calvin influence the Protestant Reformation in Europe?

8. How did Gaspard de Coligny help the Protestants of France, the Huguenots?

9. What was the St. Bartholomew's Day Massacre?

10. How did Renée, Duchess of Ferrara, help Protestant reformers?

11. Describe how did Fanino Fanini faced the sentence of death for his faith.

12. Explain why Fanini in Italy was martyred for his Evangelical faith, but Luther in Saxony, Germany, enjoyed a long life of fruitful public ministry and died a natural death.

PART FOUR

THE REFORMATION
IN ENGLAND

In 1517, students and professors at Cambridge University read and discussed the works of Erasmus, especially his edition of the Greek New Testament, making fertile ground for the writings of Martin Luther. Thomas Bilney, a Cambridge professor, was among the first to feel the joy of knowing his sins were completely forgiven through Christ's sacrifice on the cross. Bilney led many students and professors to faith in Jesus Christ. William Tyndale, banned in England from translating the Scriptures into English, fled the kingdom and did his work in hiding in Europe. His English New Testament was smuggled back into England and transformed the country.

King Henry VIII opposed the Reformation in England and instigated a brutal persecution to stamp it out. However, when he wanted a divorce from his first wife——and the pope refused to grant it——Henry separated the English church from the Church of Rome. Reformers like Thomas Cranmer and Hugh Latimer prodded Henry to permit the reformation of the church. It was an uphill battle until Henry died and his Evangelical son, Edward VI, ascended the throne. During Edward's reign, the English Reformation leapt forward, but when he died at the age of fifteen, his Roman Catholic half-sister Mary was crowned queen. She tried to reestablish the Church of Rome in England and persecuted the Protestants, ordering three hundred of them burned at the stake. When she died after a five-year reign, her Protestant half-sister Elizabeth came to the throne. Elizabeth restored the Church of England to the Evangelical faith.

CHAPTER 21:
THOMAS BILNEY

First Evangelist of the English Reformation
(c. 1495–1531)

A round the year 1519, Thomas Bilney, a short and slight university instructor, paced in front of a house on a side street in Cambridge, England. His heart raced as he tried to buck up the courage to break the law by buying a contraband book. He had been this close before, but fear of imprisonment had kept him from doing the deed. But now, out of desperation, he knocked on the door of the house. "Erasmus's New Testament," he said as he handed money to a man at the door. A minute later, Bilney, with the banned book tucked under his arm, raced back to his room at Trinity Hall.

These were the days when the writings of Martin Luther, the German reformer, swept across Europe, leading people to the Word of God and pointing them to Christ. Young King Henry VIII of

England ordered Luther's writings publicly burned and made it clear that English supporters of Luther's ideas would face persecution. But book burnings and threats did not stop the ideas of the German Reformation from spreading.

These ideas found fertile ground at Cambridge University where a revival of classical learning led many scholars to seek knowledge from original sources. This "New Learning" expanded in Cambridge when Erasmus, the Dutch scholar and theologian, taught there for several years. Erasmus inspired his students to study the New Testament in its original Greek.

Shortly after Erasmus left Cambridge in 1514, he produced a Greek New Testament compiled from the best sources and included a new and more accurate Latin translation of the New Testament. Church leaders in England, fearful that the Greek New Testament might spawn Lutheran ideas, banned the book. Despite the ban, Erasmus's New Testament was smuggled into England and sold secretly. When Thomas Bilney got his copy home, his hands trembled as he began to read it. For years, Bilney had exhausted himself and his money seeking to find peace with God through the guidance of the church. He fasted, disciplined his body, bought pardons, went daily to mass and confessed his sins to priests, but still his guilt and despair remained. But as soon as he started to read the Scriptures, God opened his eyes. He discovered a welcoming Savior who delighted to save sinners, not an aloof judge. "At last I heard Jesus," Bilney said. "Christ alone saves His people from their sins. I came to Christ. O mighty power of the Most High! God's instruction and inward working did so exhilarate my despairing heart that my bruised bones leapt for joy."

Although he did not proclaim it from the rooftops, Bilney could not keep the good news to himself. Whenever he was in conversation, he urged others to put their faith in Jesus Christ. "Christ," he said, "Christ alone saves His people from their sins."

Before long, students and lecturers crowded into his study to hear him read and comment on passages from the New Testament. For the first time, they saw Christ directly through the Scriptures and not through the eyes of church tradition. Suddenly, Christ felt close and personal. They heard the Savior preaching the good news on the mountainsides of Galilee. They saw Him calm the sea, heal the sick, embrace little children, endure the cross and rise triumphant from the tomb. Through it all, they heard Christ calling, "Come unto me all you who are weary and heavy laden and I will give you rest."

Many put their trust in the work of the living Savior and rejoiced in a new-found freedom from guilt and sin. This was the beginning of the English Reformation, an awakening of human hearts by the Spirit of God that spread from Cambridge to every corner of the kingdom.

As Bilney and his friends studied the Scriptures together, they saw the vast chasm that separated the teachings of Christ from the doctrines and practices of the Church of Rome. The church's system of salvation which emphasized priestly pardons, saints, pilgrimages and centuries of suffering in purgatory seemed very far from the Bible's simple promise: "Believe on the Lord Jesus Christ, and you shall be saved."

In the spring of 1524, students and teachers, including Bilney, packed Great St. Mary's, the University Church of Cambridge, to hear Hugh Latimer. Latimer was a tall priest and a professor known for his unquestioning loyalty to the Church of Rome. Encouraged by Bilney, a few Cambridge professors had embraced the Reformation. They taught their students to read the Scriptures for themselves, and a growing number believed in Christ for the forgiveness of their sins. Latimer publicly denounced these professors, disrupted their lectures and warned students, "Don't be deceived by these heretics!"

It was no surprise that Latimer preached against the German Reformation to the crowded church. Mocking the idea that the Scripture alone should be the Christian's supreme authority, he cautioned his hearers not to stray from the traditions of the Roman church and the rule of the pope.

While Bilney listened to Latimer's tirade, he sighed and said to himself, "I was once just like that——full of zeal without knowledge." Before the sermon ended, Bilney decided to tell Latimer that sinners could find forgiveness and eternal life only by trusting Christ. It was dangerous to approach Latimer directly; it might lead to arrest and execution as a heretic. Then Bilney hit upon a clever plan. He went to Latimer's office and asked, "Master Latimer, for the sake of God, would you hear my confession?"

Latimer, certain that his sermon must have shown the ringleader of the Cambridge reformers his errors, said to Bilney, "Please come in." Thomas Bilney knelt on the floor and said, "Let me tell you what happened to my heart and if I am in error, I am ready to be better instructed. For years, I did everything in my power to obey the commandments of God and the teachings of the church, but my guilt and sin remained. I went to mass daily and visited priest after priest to confess my sins. I followed their guidance to fast, to hold vigils and to buy pardons until I had no strength left. Nothing relieved me of the sharp sting of my sin. I was a sick and languishing soul."

Then Bilney told Latimer how he bought Erasmus's Greek New Testament. The first thing he read was a sentence from Paul's first letter to Timothy: "Christ Jesus came into the world to save sinners, of whom I am the worst." Paul thought himself the worst of sinners, but he knew he was saved in Christ. Paul believed that Christ had accomplished everything for him through his death on the cross.

"That one sentence from Paul," Bilney told him, "gave sweet comfort to my soul! My wounded heart, weighed down with guilt, leaped for joy. I looked to Christ and believed that in Him I would not perish but have everlasting life."

Latimer sat in stunned silence. This heretic was not at all as Latimer had imagined him. He was a devout man who had tried everything the church could offer to find peace with God. Then he found forgiveness in Christ by reading the Scriptures. Latimer had never heard the good news of Jesus Christ so simply explained.

Hugh Latimer became Bilney's constant companion. They met for Bible study and prayer. Latimer discovered that Bilney often prayed straight through the night, pleading with God to save sinners. The two walked the countryside around Cambridge and discussed the Scriptures. Latimer joined Bilney on his daily outreach into the city. For as soon as Bilney had turned to Christ, he felt compelled to follow in His Savior's steps by serving others. They brought food to the poor, visited prisoners in jail and went outside of town to the shacks where people suffering from contagious diseases had been banished. While changing their bandages and washing their sores, Bilney and Latimer told them of Christ's love for sinners.

Bilney introduced him to the growing circle of awakened Christians at Cambridge who met at the White Horse, an inn near the colleges, to discuss theology and encourage one another in the Lord. Students derisively called the White Horse "Little Germany," mocking the ideas of Luther that the men embraced.

Then Bilney began to leave Cambridge to preach in various places and speak out against the errors of the church that kept people from seeing Christ. Twice while he was preaching, angry priests seized him and dragged him from the pulpit. Soon Cardinal Wolsey, the most powerful churchman in the country, heard of Bilney's preaching and ordered his arrest. In November 1527, he stood trial in London before Wolsey and nine other bishops at the Chapter House in Westminster Abbey. They accused him of preaching that people are saved by faith in Christ alone, and that Christians should only pray to God and not to the saints. They charged him with teaching that it was useless to buy indulgences, go on pilgrimages and light candles before images in church. After a few days of questioning, the bishops declared him a heretic.

However, they didn't want to put him to death. They hoped to hurt the Reformation in England by getting Bilney to recant and publicly seek forgiveness for his false teaching. "Will you return to the church and revoke your heresies which you have preached?" a bishop asked him.

"I will not be untrue to the gospel," Bilney said. "I don't believe that Christ condemns what I have preached."

Over several days, the bishops badgered him to recant. And Bilney's friends begged him to yield in order to save his life. Finally, he took their advice and signed a statement that apologized for his teachings. As penance, the bishops made him carry a large bundle of sticks on his shoulders and walk to St. Paul's Cathedral. The sticks served as a reminder that he would be burned at the stake if he ever returned to his heresies. Bilney had to stand at St. Paul's Cross holding the sticks while a preacher gave a sermon, warning against any teaching that was not sanctioned by the church. Afterward, Wolsey locked him in the Tower of London for a year and then released him.

Believing that he had committed the unforgiveable sin, Bilney returned to Cambridge overwhelmed with sorrow for having denied his faith. "We stayed with him day and night," Latimer later said, "to comfort him as best we could, but he wouldn't receive it. When we quoted comforting passages of Scripture to him, it was as though we were thrusting a sword into his heart. He thought that the whole Scriptures were against him."

After nearly a year of despair, Bilney accepted the Lord's forgiveness again and felt anew the forgiving grace of God. Full of joy, he shared Christ with anyone who would listen. In 1531, Bilney decided to go out from Cambridge and preach the good news of Jesus which he had denied before the bishops. "I am going up to Jerusalem," he told his friends. They knew he meant that he was going to publicly proclaim Christ and die for his faith. He set out preaching in houses and fields. "Leave your idolatry to saints," he proclaimed. "Our Savior Christ is our mediator between us and the Father." Wherever he went, he gave away copies of William Tyndale's English New Testament which was banned by the king and bishops.

In Norwich, while Bilney brought a woman a copy of the English New Testament, officers sent from the bishop arrested him and threw him into prison. Churchmen ordered him to recant. But this time Bilney's faith in God remained unshakeable. The bishop handed him over to the sheriff for execution.

On the night before he was to be burned to death, a few friends came to visit him. One of them remarked that he was surprised to see him so cheerful and happy. "Well," Bilney said, "I will soon have unspeakable joy in heaven."

The next morning, guards led him outside the city to a place called the Lollards' Pit. He confessed his faith in Christ to the spectators who had gathered to watch him burn. Then he knelt, prayed and recited Psalm 143. When the executioner lit the fire, Bilney called out, "Jesus, I believe." Minutes later, Thomas Bilney, the first great evangelist of the English Reformation, was dead.

Hugh Latimer mourned the loss of his friend. "Bilney was God's instrument to call me to know Him," Latimer said. "I thank Bilney next to God for the knowledge that I have in the Word of God—Little Bilney, that blessed martyr of God."

CHAPTER 22:
WILLIAM TYNDALE

The Bible for the Ploughboy
(c. 1494–1536)

In 1522, William Tyndale, a young chaplain, stood preaching to a small crowd gathered on the village green in Bristol, England. Although Tyndale held degrees from the universities of Oxford and Cambridge, he did not use complicated words or talk down to people as most educated clergymen did. He spoke clearly and simply, and he spoke in earnest as one who viewed their souls as precious in the sight of God. "There is good news in the Word of God," he told them, "good, merry and joyful tidings that make a man's heart glad and make him sing, dance and leap for joy. Christ saves sinners. It is not your faith or love that wins God's favor. God loved us first and gave His Son for us, that we might see love and love in return."

Tyndale cited passages from Scripture, showing that forgiveness comes only through faith in Christ, not through penance prescribed by priests or pardons proclaimed by popes. "One of his hearers——a churchman fed up with Tyndale's habit of quoting the Bible——shouted, "We would be better off without God's law than the pope's!"

"I defy the pope and all his laws," Tyndale said. "If God spares my life, in a few years a ploughboy shall know more of the Scriptures than you do."

William Tyndale was a brilliant linguist who came to a living faith in Christ by reading the Greek New Testament. As he studied the Scriptures for himself, he found many of the church's teachings contrary to the Bible, clouding the sinner's path to Christ. He led other students to Christ by studying the Word of God with them in Greek and Latin. However, only scholars understood these languages. "The only way to lead the people to God's truth," Tyndale said, "is to lay before their eyes the Scripture in their mother tongue. He decided to translate the Bible into simple English that the common people of Britain could understand.

At that time, English law prohibited anyone from translating the Scriptures without permission of a bishop, under penalty of death. Tyndale went to the bishop of London to get his approval to translate the New Testament into English. When the bishop refused, Tyndale began to translate it in secret, but he knew that no printer in England would dare print it. And he was now a marked man because the bishop of London had convinced King Henry VIII that Tyndale was a dangerous heretic. Government agents fanned out across the kingdom with orders to arrest him. "Alas," Tyndale said, "is there no place where I can translate the Bible? All of England is closed to me."

So early in 1524, Tyndale disguised himself and fled to Germany. He went to Wittenberg, Martin Luther's city, the center of the Reformation in Europe. Tyndale got advice and help from Luther and Melanchthon. In Germany, he completed his English translation of the New Testament and found a printer in Cologne to publish it. But early in the printing process, Tyndale learned that spies of the king of England had discovered his whereabouts. Grabbing as many printed sheets as he could carry, Tyndale escaped into the night, barely avoiding capture.

He fled to another German city and found a new printer. By spring 1526, thousands of copies of Tyndale's New Testament, hidden in shipments of wheat and linen, reached the ports of Britain. The price was cheap enough that even the poor could buy a copy. Tyndale's translation used simple, down-to-earth words that everyone could understand. Soon, scholars and sailors, noblemen and nursemaids, fishmongers and farmers read the good news of Jesus Christ in English. Many trusted Christ for the forgiveness of their sins and resolved to honor Him with their lives. "The Spirit of God Himself, speaking through Scripture," Tyndale said, "gives faith to His children."

Although King Henry condemned the book, warned merchants not to ship it and threatened book dealers not to sell it, the New Testament spread across Britain from Portsmouth to Aberdeen. The bishop of London declared Tyndale's work a "wicked heresy." At Paul's Cross, outside St. Paul's Cathedral in London, he made a bonfire from seized copies of the English New Testament. When Tyndale learned of the burning of the Scripture, he said, "I expected they would burn the New Testament, and they may one day burn me also. I am content to do my duty before God."

Before long, the authorities arrested hundreds of people for having the English New Testament, and burned some at the stake for it.

But the persecution did not stop the spread of the book. "Christ is with us until the world's end," Tyndale wrote to the persecuted believers. "Let His little flock be bold therefore. For if God be on our side, it doesn't matter who is against us, be they bishops, cardinals, popes, or whatsoever."

Meanwhile, Tyndale, hunted like an outlaw, lived in hiding under false names and moved from city to city across Germany and the Low Countries——staying one step ahead of his pursuers. With the New Testament completed, he started translating the Old Testament into English. After nearly three years of labor, Tyndale went to Antwerp to oversee the printing of the first five books of the Old Testament. However, in January 1529, Tyndale got word that agents of the king were in the city searching for him. He quickly boarded a ship for Germany, but off the coast of Holland, a terrible storm broke out, whipping the waters of the North Sea to a frenzy, destroying the mast and driving the helpless ship upon the rocks. Tyndale and the other passengers narrowly escaped drowning by jumping into the frigid water and scrambling to shore.

In a few minutes, waves battered the ship to pieces. As Tyndale stood helpless and shivering on the beach, he watched the swirling waters sweep all his books and the labor of three years of translation out to sea.

Downcast but not despairing, Tyndale boarded the next ship to Hamburg and struggled to start over again. His spirits lifted when his old college friend, John Frith, escaped England and came to Germany to help him. For several months, Tyndale, with Frith's help, translated the first five books of the Old Testament again and got them printed. By the summer of 1530, they were being read in Britain.

In addition to Bible translation, Tyndale wrote several books that exposed errors in the teachings of the Roman church. He pointed his readers to the Word of God for their rule of faith, not church leaders. "Christ's church," Tyndale wrote, "is all repenting sinners that believe in Christ and put their trust in the mercy of God."

Many people accepted the teachings of the church that said by performing religious rituals and doing good works, believers contributed to their salvation. "Nothing can save us except faith in Christ alone," Tyndale warned. "If you are surrounded by a thousand holy candles and a hundred tons of holy water and have a ship full of pardons and perform all the ceremonies in the world and do all the good works of all the men in the world——it will not make you holy before God."

He urged everyone to cling to Christ and not to lose heart when they sinned. "If through our weakness we fall a thousand times a day," Tyndale said, "yet if we repent again, we will always find abundant mercy in Christ Jesus our Lord."

The English Scripture and Tyndale's books accelerated the Reformation in England. Not only did the common people find new faith in Christ and enjoy close fellowship with their Savior, but many priests, monks and nuns put their trust in Christ alone. This alarmed the king and the bishops who feared these changes would weaken their hold on the people. They banned all of Tyndale's writings in the kingdom. "Tyndale must be captured," said Thomas More, King Henry's chief official. "I will not leave Tyndale the darkest corner in which to hide his head."

While Tyndale and Frith labored on the continent, church officials in England captured their dear friend and mentor, Thomas Bilney, when he brought a friend the English New Testament. They burned him at the stake for his Evangelical preaching.

In the summer of 1532, Frith felt compelled to return to England to preach Christ. Tyndale warned him that it was too dangerous, but he went anyway. After a few months, John Frith was captured and burned at the stake. The news of Frith's death hit William Tyndale like a hammer blow. He sought the Lord's comfort in prayer with tears. But Tyndale knew the Scriptures, and he did not grieve like those who have no hope. Meanwhile, the net of persecution tightened around him. Prodded by the pope, Emperor Charles V sought to stamp out the Reformation that was rapidly expanding in the Low Countries where Tyndale lived in hiding. Charles ordered the execution of all preachers and followers of the Evangelical faith and all printers of the Scriptures.

In May 1535, an English spy who had befriended Tyndale led him into a trap. Officers of the emperor captured him and hauled him to Vilvorde Castle near Brussels. They threw Tyndale into a foul-smelling dungeon. For eighteen months, he worked in his frigid and dark cell, writing papers defending his beliefs from the Bible. His threadbare clothes failed to keep out the bone-chilling cold. He suffered from headaches, chest congestion and a chronic cough. A steady stream of churchmen and inquisitors came to question, harangue and threaten him. Tyndale endured it all with such patience and kindness that he won the heart of the jailor who turned to Christ. "If Tyndale is not a true Christian," one worker in the castle said, "there is no such thing."

When the authorities at last brought Tyndale to trial, they charged him with teaching that sinners are justified by faith alone, that all who believe and embrace the forgiveness of sins in Jesus Christ are saved, that there is no purgatory, that prayers must be offered to God alone and not to the Virgin Mary or the saints. "You pervert the Scriptures to spread your heresies," they said.

"I call God to record against the day we shall appear before our Lord Jesus," Tyndale replied, "that I never altered one syllable of God's Word."

Tyndale told his accusers that his beliefs came from his study of the Scriptures and that unless they could show him from the Bible that he was wrong, he would never recant. The judges quickly rendered a guilty verdict.

In October 1536, guards led William Tyndale out of the castle and tied him to a stake. Just before they put him to death, Tyndale said aloud, "Lord, open the king of England's eyes."

Shortly thereafter, King Henry VIII permitted the use of the Bible in English and ordered every church in England to have an English Bible for the congregation to read. Within a few years of Tyndale's death, at a gathering of English churchmen, one bishop declared, "The people now know the Holy Scripture better than many of us."

The New Testament of the King James Bible used Tyndale's translation nearly word for word. The beliefs he died for became the foundation of Protestant churches around the world. His example of unflinching faith in Christ, undying love for the Scriptures and unwavering work for the kingdom of God will never be forgotten.

REFORMATION   BASICS   6

The Sacraments and the Mass

The medieval church proclaimed a system of seven sacraments through which the church claimed to dispense God's grace. It had also developed the sacrifice of the mass, wherein Christ was ritually offered up to God the Father in the worship service. The reformers rejected the Church of Rome's teaching on the sacraments and the mass. They taught that Christ died once and for all on the cross and could not be sacrificed and offered anew to the Father in the mass.

The reformers taught that Christ had instituted only two sacraments, baptism and the Lord's Supper. They rejected the Roman Catholic understanding of the Lord's Supper known as transubstantiation which stated that the bread and wine of the sacrament miraculously became the physical body and blood of Jesus. Although the reformers did not all agree on the precise meaning of the Lord's Supper, they all rejected transubstantiation.

The Heidelberg Catechism question and answer 80 typifies what the reformers generally believed about the Lord's Supper and the mass.

> What difference is there between the Lord's Supper and the popish mass?

> Answer: The Lord's supper testifies to us, that we have a full pardon of all sin by the only sacrifice of Jesus Christ, which he himself has once accomplished on the cross; and, that we by the Holy Ghost are ingrafted into Christ, who,

according to his human nature is now not on earth, but in heaven, at the right hand of God his Father, and will there be worshipped by us. But the mass teaches, that the living and dead have not the pardon of sins through the sufferings of Christ, unless Christ is also daily offered for them by the priests; and further, that Christ is bodily under the form of bread and wine, and therefore is to be worshipped in them; so that the mass, at bottom, is nothing else than a denial of the one sacrifice and sufferings of Jesus Christ, and an accursed idolatry."

CHAPTER 23:
JOHN FRITH

English Martyr for Christ and His Word
(1503–1533)

In February 1528, Cardinal Wolsey, the most powerful churchman in England and the king's highest official, cast ten Oxford
University students into a dungeon. Their crime: they studied
together the Greek New Testament, discussed the false teachings
of the church and urged students to turn to the risen Christ for the
forgiveness of their sins. Church leaders feared that such activities
would undermine their authority. One of the men was John Frith,
a mathematician and language scholar who found Christ while
studying at Cambridge University through the testimony of William Tyndale and other Cambridge reformers like Thomas Bilney.

The dungeon, a dark cellar, deep underground of Cardinal College, reeked of the salted fish stored there. Water oozed from the

walls and floor, and the damp, cold air infected the students' lungs. For six months, their only food was salted fish. The young men, emaciated by malnutrition and racked with fever, wasted away. By August, four of them had died.

Cardinal Wolsey——afraid that the deaths of so many young men would turn the people against him and the church——ordered the release of the surviving prisoners. He restricted their travel until they came to trial. John Frith escaped, crossed the North Sea and joined William Tyndale in the Low Countries. Tyndale was translating the Bible into English so that the common people of Britain could understand it. Since the English church and state forbade him from translating the Scriptures into English, he fled to the continent and did his work there. By 1526, copies of Tyndale's New Testament in English were smuggled into England. King Henry VIII banned the book and sent agents to Europe to arrest Tyndale. So Tyndale lived in hiding as he worked on an English translation of the Old Testament. In 1529, John Frith arrived to help him. "There is no one I trust more," Tyndale said of him, "not only for his learning but also for his heart for God."

Frith informed Tyndale about the progress of the Reformation in Britain. He told him about the burning of Patrick Hamilton, the Scottish reformer, the year before. Frith brought with him Hamilton's Latin manuscript which explained the basic teachings of the Evangelical faith. Frith translated it into English and entitled it: *Patrick's Places.* He had it printed and smuggled back to England and Scotland.

For several months, Tyndale, with Frith's help, wrapped up his translation of the first five books of the Old Testament. In addition to Bible translation, Tyndale and Frith wrote several books that exposed errors in the church and called readers to be reconciled to

God through Christ's death. "If we believe that out of God's mercy, He gave His most dear Son to redeem us from our sin," Frith wrote, "and if we believe that He does not impute our sins to us, but that His wrath is pacified in Christ and His blood… then, we are righteous in His sight, and our conscience is at peace with God——not through ourselves but through our Lord Jesus Christ."

The English Scripture and the books of Tyndale and Frith rapidly advanced the Reformation in England. Even though they learned of fierce persecution in England——including the burning of their friend, Thomas Bilney——Frith felt compelled to return to his homeland and preach Christ to his countrymen. Tyndale feared that Frith would be killed for his faith there and pled with his friend not to go.

In the summer of 1532, John Frith arrived in London. He met with Evangelicals who gathered secretly. Frith told them to look to Christ as He is found in the Scriptures. "I pray God will increase your knowledge of His Word," he said. "I do not want any man to accept my words unless they stand with the Scripture and are approved by Scripture. Try them with God's Word."

At one meeting, someone asked Frith about his opinion of the Lord's Supper. Frith did not want to talk about the disagreements that Evangelicals had over the Lord's Supper. He wanted to focus on Christ's death and resurrection for sinners. But when pressed, Frith carefully explained that he believed the Scriptures teach that Christ is spiritually present in the sacrament to those who received Him by faith. "Our bishops think differently," said one man. "They believe that the bread, transformed by the priest's consecration, becomes the flesh, blood and bones of Christ, and that we must adore the host. Please write down your thoughts on the sacrament for me, for I am afraid I will not remember what you have said."

So Frith wrote an explanation from the Scriptures about the meaning of the Lord's Supper. "We must eat and drink the body and blood of Christ, not with the teeth," he wrote, "but with hearing through faith." Frith asked the man not to show the paper to others, but he found Frith's argument so true to the Scriptures that he shared it with his friends. Eventually, a copy of it landed in the hands of Sir Thomas More, King Henry VIII's Lord Chancellor, a persecutor of reformers.

When More heard that Frith was in England, he sent agents in search of him and notified every town and seaport to be on the lookout for him, promising a large reward for Frith's capture. Aware that he was a hunted man, Frith disguised himself, traveled under assumed names and moved from place to place. In October 1532, as the danger of capture increased, Frith decided to slip out of England. He traveled to the English Channel, hoping to set sail for Europe. When he tried to board a ship, agents of the king arrested him and threw him into the Tower of London.

The zeal of Frith, Tyndale and the other reformers perplexed Thomas More. "These diabolical people," More said, "print books at great expense, notwithstanding the great danger——not looking for any gain, they give them away to everybody. They fear no labor, no expense, no pain, no danger and no injury."

For five months, Frith languished in the Tower. Despite repeated interrogations and threats, he refused to recant. "Stand fast and commit yourself to God," Tyndale wrote him in a letter.

The authorities told Frith that his books and Tyndale's reeked of heresy. "Master Tyndale and I have made this offer many times," Frith said. "If you will allow the English Bible to be printed and used in England, then my brother William Tyndale and I will promise you to write no more."

"Tyndale is a heretic, a son of the devil," a bishop told Frith.

"Tyndale's understanding of Scripture makes him more worthy to be honored than all the bishops in England," Frith replied.

In his jail cell, without the use of a Bible or any books, he wrote papers defending his beliefs from the Word of God and the writings of the early church fathers. He also sent letters of encouragement to Evangelicals outside the prison walls. "Imitators of the Lord," he wrote them, "bear the cross as soon as God shall be pleased to send it."

Archbishop Cranmer, a supporter of the Reformation, did everything in his power to save Frith, but King Henry, Thomas More and the bishop of London insisted that he recant or die. When the bishops demanded a hearing of Frith's case in order to condemn him to death, Cranmer arranged the meeting to take place at his country estate outside of London. Archbishop Cranmer sent an Evangelical gentleman and one of his trusted aides to fetch him from the Tower. Cranmer's men encouraged Frith to compromise his teachings a little. "If you do," one told him, "you will be free to serve the Lord in the future."

"Mr. Frith," the gentleman said, "if you are not prudent, you are lost. What a pity! You are so learned in Latin and Greek and the Holy Scriptures, the ancient doctors and all kinds of knowledge. You will perish, and all your admirable gifts will perish with you, with little profit to the world, and less comfort to your wife and children, your kinfolk and friends."

Frith thanked him for his kindness but said he must be faithful to the true doctrine of the Lord. "And," Frith added, "if I am fairly tried, I shall have nothing to fear."

"Indeed!" said the gentleman. "If you are fairly tried, you would be safe, but that is what I very much doubt. Our Master

Christ was not fairly tried, nor would He be, if He were present again in the world."

"I must be true to my conscience," Frith told them, "although I should lose my life twenty times over. I can support my teachings from the Holy Scriptures and the ancient fathers of the church. God will help me."

As they walked through pastures and woodlands, it became clear that Frith would not compromise his beliefs, but Archbishop Cranmer's men had come with a back-up plan to save him. "Mr. Frith," the gentleman said, "we have a way for your escape."

"Run east into Kent," he said. "That is your home country where you have many friends. We will wait here a few hours so you can make your escape. Then we will go and raise a hue and cry to the nearest constable and tell him that you fled westward."

Frith smiled and said, "If you leave me here and report that you have lost me, I will follow after you as fast as I can and bring the news that I had found Frith and brought him back again."

"You are mad," the gentleman cried out. "Do you think your reasoning will convert the bishops? Why don't you escape across the sea as you have done before?"

"My conscience binds me to defend the teachings for which I am persecuted," Frith told him. "If I should run away now, I would be running from my God. I must bear testimony to His Holy Word."

Not long after, Frith stood trial at St. Paul's Cathedral before the bishop of London. When Frith refused to recant his beliefs, the bishop declared him an outcast from Christ's church and condemned him to death by burning. "No matter what you say," Frith said, "I know that I am Christ's."

Guards cast him into Newgate prison to await execution. Tyndale wrote Frith one last letter, "Commit yourself completely to your most loving Father and most kind Lord. Your cause is Christ's gospel, a light that must be fed with the blood of faith. Your wife is well content with the will of God."

A few days later, a guard threw into his cell a twenty-four-year-old tailor named Andrew Hewitt. Frith asked him what crime he committed to be sent to prison. "I was brought before the bishops and asked about my beliefs," he said. "I told them, 'I think as Frith does.' Then the bishop of London said, 'Why, Frith is a heretic and already condemned to be burned, and if you do not retract your opinion you shall be burned with him.'

'I am content,' I told them. So they sent me here to be burned along with you."

On July 4, 1533, the lord mayor of London and his guards led Frith and Hewitt from the prison to the execution site in Smithfield. At the stake, a minister preached a message, condemning Frith's beliefs. Then looking over the crowd, he shouted, "And let none of you people pray for these dogs!"

When the preacher finished, Frith smiled at him and said, "May the Lord forgive you."

Then Frith and Hewitt committed their souls to God and died for their faith.

CHAPTER 24:
HUGH LATIMER

Foremost Preacher of the English Reformation
(1485–1555)

In the early 1520s, when King Henry VIII of England waged war against the Protestant Reformation, Hugh Latimer supported him wholeheartedly. Latimer, a tall priest and a Cambridge University professor known for his unquestioning loyalty to the Church of Rome, cautioned his college students not to stray from the Roman church. He publicly denounced reformed-minded instructors like Thomas Bilney, disrupting their lectures and warning their students, "Don't be deceived by these heretics!"

All that changed in the spring of 1524, when Thomas Bilney came to his room and asked Latimer to hear his confession. Bilney wanted to tell Latimer about Christ's great love for sinners. He explained how for many years he strove with all his might to obey the commandments of God and the teachings of the church, but his guilt and sin remained. Then he told Latimer how he began to read the Greek New Testament. Those words, he told Latimer with his face beaming, "gave sweet comfort to my soul! My wounded heart, weighed down with guilt, leapt for joy. I saw that all my vigils, my fasts, my pilgrimages, my purchase of masses and indulgences were destroying instead of saving me. I looked to Christ and believed that in Him I would not perish, but have everlasting life."

Latimer suddenly saw the reformers in a new light. They were not heretics, but devout men who found forgiveness in Christ by reading the Scriptures and believing them. Although Hugh Latimer did not admit it at the time, he too, had an uneasy conscience. His fear of death and damnation had often led him to consider becoming a monk to win God's favor. Latimer had never heard the gospel so simply explained. "I learned more by hearing his confession," Latimer said later, "than I had before in many years. From that time onward, I began to seek the Word of God."

He got a copy of the New Testament and began to devour it. Latimer saw that it was not what the church performed on his behalf or what he did for himself that mattered, but what Christ did for him. Soon, he put all his hope of forgiveness and eternal life into the hands of his Savior, Jesus Christ. He was a changed man, a new creation in Christ. Before, he had looked to the church and found fasting, penance, priestly absolution and despair. Now, he looked to Christ and found grace, forgiveness, peace and joy.

Hugh Latimer began to join Bilney each day for Bible study and prayer. With his new friend, Latimer brought food to the poor, cared for the sick and visited prisoners in jail, telling them all about Christ's love for sinners. Latimer began to preach in the churches of Cambridge the faith he had once tried to destroy. He surprised his hearers and led many to the Lord. "Whereas before he was an enemy and almost a persecutor of Christ," one observer said, "he now was a zealous seeker after Him."

From the start, Latimer understood the Bible's most important truth: salvation is a gift of God's free grace through Christ's victory on the cross. He made it the focal point of all his preaching. "Christ came to deliver us from sin and damnation," he preached. "Christ gave his body to be torn upon the cross for that. Neither could any work or law or sacrifice redeem us from that but Christ only."

Latimer made it clear that Christ opened his arms wide to welcome even the vilest sinner. "Though one man had done all the world's sins since Adam's time," he preached, "yet he may be remedied by the blood of Jesus Christ. If he believes in Him, he shall be cleansed from all his sins. The grace and mercies of God far exceeds our sins."

As he went around the kingdom preaching that Jesus fully paid the price for all the sins of everyone who believes in Him, he became known as the boldest preacher in the land. Latimer called people to trust in Christ and to serve others, especially the needy. At that time, noblemen were expelling tenant farmers from lands that had been tilled by their families for centuries. He challenged ministers to stick up for the poor. "You preachers," Latimer advised, "must preach against covetousness. Don't fear these giants of England, these great men of power that are oppressors of the poor. The poorest ploughman that these men are abusing is in Christ equal with the greatest prince in the kingdom."

Latimer's preaching made many enemies. Churchmen hated him for exposing their sin. The rich chafed when he pointed out their mistreatment of the poor. His detractors called him "a knave and a heretic." One man vowed, "If Latimer were to be burned as a heretic, I would carry a bundle of sticks sixteen miles to add fuel to the fire."

But many loved him. A nobleman who found Christ through Latimer's preaching said, "I have an ear for other preachers, but I have a heart for Latimer."

In the 1530s, when King Henry VIII wanted to loosen the pope's grip on the church in England, he turned to the reformers for help. He made Thomas Cranmer archbishop of Canterbury and appointed Hugh Latimer bishop of Worcester. Cranmer and Latimer urged Henry to support an English translation of the New Testament and make it widely available. Latimer pressed the king to do it quickly. "I pray your Highness," he wrote the king, "do it today. Don't wait for tomorrow." Eventually, Henry allowed the Scriptures in English to be printed and sold throughout the land.

Unlike most bishops who spent their time in their palaces or in London, Latimer visited the ministers and congregations of his diocese. When he discovered that the ministers knew almost nothing of the Scriptures, he saw to it that each minister had a Bible. He required them to read and study at least one chapter every day. Latimer called them to preach faithfully and to encourage their flock to read the Scriptures for themselves.

Although Henry separated the church in England from the control of the pope and allowed the use of English Bibles, he held tightly to the teaching and practices of the Roman church and prevented the reformers from making the English church more faithful to the teachings of the Scriptures. In 1539, Henry had Parliament pass a law that required all ministers to subscribe to several beliefs that many found contrary to the Scriptures. Latimer refused to agree to them, and he resigned as bishop. When a friend asked him why, he said, "I am resolved to be guided only by the Word of God, and sooner than depart one jot from that, let me be trampled under the feet of wild horses."

Henry had him arrested and thrown into the Tower of London. When the king released him, he banned Latimer from preaching. Eight years later, when Henry died, his son Edward VI came to the throne and a great movement to reform the church in England began. Latimer received a license to preach anywhere in the kingdom. He traveled far and wide, proclaiming the living Christ and the doctrines of Scripture.

When Edward VI died in 1553, his Roman Catholic half-sister Mary became queen. She launched a vicious persecution of Evangelicals as she tried to return England to the Roman church. Protestant bishops were removed from office, and many were imprisoned. Hundreds of Protestant preachers fled the country. Latimer could have escaped, but he wanted to bear witness to his faith.

Officials of the queen arrested him and imprisoned him in the Tower of London. When Latimer arrived at the Tower, he met on the green one of the guards whom he recognized from the time Henry VIII had cast him in the Tower. "My old friend," Latimer said to him, "how are you doing? I have come to be your neighbor again." It was winter, and he was locked in a frigid cell with no fire to warm him. The bone-chilling cold caused his body to shiver and ache. "They plan to burn me," he told his jailer, "but if I don't get some heat soon, I am likely to freeze to death first."

While in prison, Latimer spent most of the day reading the New Testament. He read it through seven times waiting for his case to be heard. And he prayed, begging God to give him the grace and strength to remain faithful. At times he knelt in prayer for so long that he could not stand up again without help. One man who spent time with him in his cell said, "Latimer prayed as though he could see God before him. He spoke as if they were face-to-face."

In the spring, the queen's council sent Latimer to Oxford University to stand trial along with his friends and fellow reformers, Thomas Cranmer, the archbishop of Canterbury, and Nicholas Ridley, the bishop of London.

A great crowd thronged St. Mary's Church in Oxford eager to witness the trial of the famous bishops. Ridley and Latimer were tried first before a tribunal of church officials and university professors. The chief accuser, putting on a concerned expression, rose and approached the white-haired, seventy-year-old Latimer saying, "Master Latimer, for God's love, consider your position. You have had the office of bishop; you are a learned man. Consider that if you die now, you die without grace, for outside the Church of Rome there can be no salvation."

Latimer's Bible hung from a leather strap on his belt; his spectacles, tied to a string around his neck, rested on his chest. Though Latimer's body was stooped with pain, he stood straight as he could and answered. "I know perfectly by God's Word that the true church is in all the world, but its foundation is not in Rome only as you say. The true church is ruled only by the Scriptures."

The churchman pointed at Ridley and Latimer and demanded, "Swear allegiance to the pope, confess your heresies and you will live." But Ridley and Latimer stood their ground and attempted to respond with biblical answers, though they were often interrupted with hisses from their accusers, who acted more like barnyard animals than scholars. After two days of hearings, the court excommunicated them from the church and turned them over to the crown for punishment. Queen Mary ordered their execution by burning. When word reached Latimer that he was to be burned at the stake as a heretic, he said, "I thank God that I might glorify Him by this kind of death."

Shortly before the sentence was carried out, the court gave Latimer one last chance to recant. "I will not deny my Master Jesus Christ and His truth," he said.

On October 16, 1555, most of Oxford gathered across from Balliol College, outside the town's north gate, to watch the executions. Ridley wore a black robe, Latimer a worn coat and buttoned cap. The two men warmly embraced when they met at the stake. Ridley smiled and said, "Be of good heart, brother, for God will either ease the pain of the flames or else strengthen us to endure it."

Latimer nodded saying, "God is faithful. He will not let you be tempted beyond what you can bear." They knelt in the dirt and prayed, then spoke quiet words of comfort to one another. A priest delivered a sermon accusing Latimer and Ridley of terrible heresies, condemning them to the fires of hell.

Guards strapped the two bishops to the stake with a single iron chain, binding them tightly around the waist, and surrounded them with straw and wood. As the bailiff stepped forward with a torch, Latimer said, "Be of good cheer, Master Ridley, and play the man. We shall this day, by God's grace, light such a candle in England, as I trust, will never be put out."

The news of their deaths swept across England. When Queen Mary died three years later in 1558, the persecution of Protestants ended and the teachings for which Latimer and Ridley and many others had died became the foundation of the Church of England.

CHAPTER 25:
THOMAS CRANMER

First Protestant Archbishop of Canterbury

(1489–1556)

In January 1547, at Whitehall Palace in London, King Henry VIII lay dying. The English monarch, who had married six times* and separated England from the Roman church, had sent for Archbishop Cranmer. Fourteen years earlier, Henry plucked Thomas Cranmer, a little-known Evangelical instructor from Cambridge University, and appointed him to the highest post in the English Church. At first, Cranmer recoiled at the thought of becoming archbishop of Canterbury. "Wretch that I am!" he said. "No man has ever desired a bishopric less than me." Cranmer was married, and Henry believed the doctrine of the Roman church that

---

* Read about Henry's sixth wife, Katherine Parr, in *Radiant: Fifty Remarkable Women in Church History* (2015).

ministers must remain single. "I see nothing but troubles, conflicts and insurmountable dangers in my path," Cranmer said.

His fears proved true. He and his fellow Evangelicals wanted to reform the Church of England according to the Scriptures, but Henry and his conservative English bishops merely wanted to break England free from the authority of the pope while keeping the basic doctrines and worship of the Roman church. While facing the daunting task of working with the headstrong king who did not hesitate to put to death those who crossed him, Cranmer patiently advocated for reform. He sought to pull the people away from their devotion to saints and images and lead them to a loving relationship with Christ. He wanted all the ministers in England to clearly proclaim that people are saved from their sins through faith in Christ alone and not by their good works. He longed to have church services in English, not Latin, so that the congregation could understand and participate in worship. When Cranmer tried to implement these reforms, Henry blocked him. Despite many setbacks, Cranmer plodded on and slowly he made headway, including installing reformers like Hugh Latimer as bishops in the church.

To get the Bible in English into the hands of the people was Cranmer's greatest goal. The reformers believed that if the Word of God became the supreme rule for the Church of England, then scriptural beliefs and practices would come in due time. "If we possess the Holy Scriptures," Cranmer said, "we have at hand a remedy for every disease. Beset as we are with tribulations and temptations, where can we find help to overcome them? In Scripture. It is the balm that will heal our wounds and will be a more precious jewel in our houses than either gold or silver."

Several years earlier, when William Tyndale's New Testament in English began to circulate in England, Henry banned it, ordered all copies to be burned and called for Tyndale's execution. But over time, Cranmer convinced Henry to allow the Bible to be published in English, overturning hundreds of years of prejudice against the people having the Scriptures in their own language. By 1538, the king required every church in the kingdom to have a copy of the Scriptures in English for the people to read. And Cranmer directed all the ministers to teach the people to recite the Lord's Prayer, the Ten Commandments and the Apostles' Creed in English. The conservative bishops and ministers rankled under the changes. "We put to death the Lollards for reading the gospel in English, and now we are ordered to teach it in that language," they complained.

Through the years, Cranmer continued to study the Scriptures and read the writings of the German and Swiss reformers. Gradually, he changed his views regarding such doctrines as purgatory and transubstantiation——the Roman church's belief that the bread and wine are transformed into the physical body and blood of Christ in the mass. Often, Cranmer did not press hard for reforms, but waited patiently for change. At other times, he stood up boldly to the king and told him that he was wrong. "It is not my own cause that I defend," Cranmer told Henry once, "it is that of Almighty God."

On several occasions, Cranmer expected to be arrested for his principled stands against the king. Once, when Cranmer thought it likely that he would be put to death for his views, he sent his wife and children out of England for their safety. Despite their differences, Henry trusted and respected Thomas Cranmer and kept him on as archbishop. And as Henry's health failed, he put Cranmer in charge of his son Edward's education and appointed an Evangelical nobleman to act as his son's regent until Edward was old enough to rule the kingdom. Under Cranmer's influence, young Edward embraced the Evangelical faith.

When Henry knew that his death was imminent, he summoned Cranmer to his palace bedside. When the archbishop arrived, he found the king very weak and unable to talk. "Your Highness," Cranmer said, "put your trust in Christ and call on Him for mercy." Cranmer took Henry's hand and said, "I know you cannot speak, but if you are trusting in Christ, give me a sign with your eyes or hand." Then the king squeezed the archbishop's hand as hard as he could. Soon after, the king died.

A few weeks later in February 1547, Henry's nine-year-old son was crowned King Edward VI. At last, the path was open for Cranmer to press forward with reforms. With the help of other Evangelicals, Cranmer wrote the *Book of Common Prayer*, a new liturgy for worship services in English. While Henry reigned, the people experienced the same worship that they had for centuries where they were largely spectators of a ritual performed by the priest. The priest spent most of the service speaking Latin before a stone altar with his back to the people.

Under Cranmer's leadership, all that changed. Now the minister faced the people and spoke English for the entire service. The congregation participated with responses and prayers in English, designed to straightforwardly present the good news of Jesus Christ. Ministers read the Scriptures and explained them in a sermon. They taught that Christ was not physically present in the bread and wine of communion as the Roman church taught, but spiritually present in the hearts of believers who received the elements by faith. Gone were petitions for souls suffering in purgatory and prayers addressed to Mary and the saints.

With the help of Nicholas Ridley, the bishop of London, and other reformers, Cranmer wrote the *Forty-two Articles* which set down the fundamental doctrines of the Christian faith. They stressed the

Scriptures as the only infallible rule of Christian faith and practice, making the Church of England thoroughly Protestant. Ministers were permitted to marry, and finally Cranmer could have his wife and children as part of his public life.

But in the summer of 1553, just as the great transformation of the Church of England took root, King Edward died. A few weeks later, his half-sister Mary, a staunch supporter of the Church of Rome, was crowned queen. Soon, she mustered all her power to drag the Church of England back under the authority of the pope, eliminating anyone who stood in the way. She restored the Latin mass and banned the English Bible. Reformed-minded ministers and bishops were removed from office, and many were arrested. Some Evangelicals renounced their faith to save their lives. Many fled the country, but not Mary's chief adversary, Thomas Cranmer. "All the doctrine and religion accepted during the reign of King Edward VI," Cranmer declared, "is more pure and according to God's Word, than any that has been used in England these thousands of years."

Within weeks of her coronation, Queen Mary's henchmen seized Archbishop Cranmer and locked him in the Tower of London where his friends Latimer and Ridley were already imprisoned. Not long after, a court sentenced Cranmer to death for treason. After suffering for months in a dark cell in the Tower, Cranmer, Latimer and Ridley were sent to Oxford University to stand trial for heresy.

At the trial, an array of academics and churchmen interrogated Cranmer, demanding that he recant his views and swear allegiance to the pope which he steadfastly refused to do. They questioned him at length regarding his beliefs about communion, calling him a heretic for refusing to believe that the bread and wine in the mass are transformed into the physical body and blood of Christ. By quoting Scripture and the early church fathers, Cranmer defended the teaching that Christ is spiritually present in the sacrament. Although the lead prosecutor called him "unlearned and impudent" and the audience booed and hissed when Cranmer replied, the old archbishop stood his ground.

After several rounds of questioning, they declared him a heretic and condemned him to death. Latimer and Ridley received the same sentence. On October 16, 1555, guards forced Cranmer to watch while his two friends burned at the stake outside the prison walls. When Cranmer saw their suffering, he wept, collapsed to his knees and prayed. But the authorities were not ready to burn Cranmer just yet. They hoped to turn him from his convictions and discredit the Reformation.

At first they threatened and abused him, but Cranmer refused to condemn the Protestant Reformation or his writings. Then his persecutors changed tactics. They transferred Cranmer from his cold cell to a comfortable room in the home of an Oxford dean. Scholars and priests lavished him with kindness, urging him to return to the Church of Rome. "Dr. Cranmer," they told him, "if you would just recant some of your views, you would win the queen's favor and be quickly restored to your great office in the church." After enduring harsh treatment for more than two years, the kindness threw Cranmer off guard. Little by little, he agreed to change his mind, until at last he signed his name to a paper which read: "I, Thomas Cranmer, late Bishop of Canterbury, do renounce all heresies and errors not in agreement with the Church of Rome. I acknowledge the pope as the supreme head of the church whom all must obey. I believe in the seven sacraments, purgatory and prayers to the saints. I am sorry that I ever thought otherwise and led others away from the Church of Rome."

Hoping to discourage the Evangelicals, church leaders printed his confession and publicized it throughout England. Yet despite his confession, Queen Mary insisted on his death and sentenced him to burn at the stake. Church officials decided that on the morning of the execution, Cranmer should speak against the Reformation and call everyone to renounce the Protestant faith.

St. Mary's University Church in Oxford overflowed with spectators who had come to hear the old archbishop speak and to watch him die. All eyes fixed on Cranmer who wore a torn, dirty robe and stood on a raised platform opposite the pulpit. He bowed his bald head as he listened to a preacher condemning the Reformation and Cranmer's part in it. "But," the preacher added, his eyes scanning the assembled throng, "Dr. Cranmer has confessed his sins and recanted his errors and he will address you now."

Cranmer knelt, sighed deeply, and prayed, "O Father, have mercy on me, most miserable sinner. I have offended against both heaven and earth, more than I can say. Have mercy upon me, O Lord, for Your great mercy." Then he rose and faced the congregation, tears brimming in his eyes. "I desire to speak a few words before I die by which God might be glorified and you instructed in the faith."

In solemn tones, he urged them to love one another and care for the poor. "And now," he said, raising his voice for all to hear, "I come to the great thing which troubles my conscience more than anything I ever did in my whole life. I now renounce the things written with my hand against the truth in my heart. I feared death. I wrote the recantation to save my life. And because my hand has offended, writing against my heart, therefore my hand shall be punished first, for when I come to the fire, it shall be burned first. And as for the pope, I refuse him as Christ's enemy with all his false doctrines."

"Stop the heretic's mouth," someone cried. Murmurs and shouts erupted throughout the church. "Lead the heretic away!" came the order. As the crowd jeered loudly, guards pulled Cranmer from the platform and rushed him through the drizzling rain to the same spot where his friends, Ridley and Latimer, died.

As the fire began to rise, Cranmer, true to his word, stretched out his right hand, held it unflinchingly in the flames and said, "This unworthy right hand——this hand has offended."

Soon he perished in the fire. But his brave witness for the Reformation at the end emboldened many Protestants to hold fast to Christ in the face of fierce persecution. Within a few years, Queen Mary died, and the Reformation was restored in England.

CHAPTER 26:
JOHN BRADFORD

The Hearty Gospeller
(1510–1555)

Early in the reign of Edward VI, a large crowd of courtiers thronged the royal court at Westminster to hear the great Protestant reformer, Hugh Latimer. The famous preacher——knowing the court was full of people who had gained wealth by cheating others——spoke directly to their sins and their need of a Savior. He preached on Christ's command to believers to make restitution to those against whom they had sinned. After the sermon, John Bradford, a tall, well-dressed young lawyer with a red beard, approached Latimer. Moved by the message and overcome by a guilty conscience, Bradford confessed that he and his former superior had defrauded the royal treasury of a large sum to his superior's benefit. Latimer advised him to contact his superior and make restitution.

For several years, Bradford had worked for John Harrington, the paymaster for King Henry VIII's army. Bradford left his employ on good terms, and Harrington paid Bradford a pension for his services. At some risk to himself, Bradford contacted Harrington and told him that they needed to make restitution. Bradford informed him that if he refused to return the money obtained by fraud, then Bradford would feel compelled to reveal the matter to the king.

Harrington reluctantly agreed to pay the restitution. He gave the money to Latimer who turned it over to the royal treasurer, withholding the name of the provider to protect Harrington. "A great weighty burden has been lifted from me," Bradford told a friend. But it cost him the goodwill of Harrington who cut off his pension payments.

The whole experience renewed Bradford's faith in Christ, and he became a disciple of Hugh Latimer. With Latimer's encouragement, he forsook the practice of law and the pursuit of wealth to prepare for the ministry. "After that," a friend said of Bradford, "God touched his heart with that holy and effectual calling. He sold his rings and jewels of gold and gave the money for the relief of Christ's poor."

Bradford went to Cambridge University to study the Scriptures and progressed so rapidly that within one year Pembroke College made him a fellow to teach and oversee students. Bradford often read the Scriptures and studied theology on his knees, making his studies a prayer to God. He worshiped with the students each morning in the college chapel and then gathered interested students in his rooms for prayer. His kindliness won the hearts of those he encountered in and out of the university.

In the summer of 1550, the bishop of London, Nicholas Ridley, ordained Bradford to the Christian ministry and made him a chaplain at St. Paul's Cathedral. "God works wonders through Master Bradford in setting forth His Word," Ridley said. King Edward VI gave him a license to preach anywhere in the kingdom. Bradford led many Englishmen to Christ for the full forgiveness of their sins, and he challenged them to live for Christ.

Shortly after the death of Edward and the crowning of his half-sister Mary, a persecution of the reformers began. Queen Mary, a devout follower of the Church of Rome, tried to sweep away the English Reformation begun during the reign of her father Henry VIII and advanced by Edward. She ordered the arrest of leading reformers like Nicholas Ridley, Thomas Cranmer and Hugh Latimer. But Bradford continued to diligently preach the doctrines of the Reformation. He knew that God's grace alone would give him and the other reformers the strength to stand firm. "These perilous days of necessity so nip us and provoke us to pray," he wrote. He said that without prayer, "we cannot bear it."

In August 1553, Bradford stood on the dais at St. Paul's Cross in London when Gilbert Bourne, a minister who renounced the Reformation when Mary came to power, preached a sermon extolling the Roman church's doctrines favored by the queen. The large crowd, boiled with indignation at his teaching, created a ruckus and tried to pull him from the pulpit and beat him. Neither the new bishop of London, nor the mayor could calm the crowd. At length Bourne, fearing for his life, begged Bradford to talk to the people. As Bradford stepped forward, a dagger thrown at Bourne brushed his sleeve and missed its intended mark.

When Bradford began to speak, the crowd quieted. "Bradford," they cried, "God save your life, Bradford!"

He preached to them, exhorting them to act with Christian patience, directing them to peacefully disperse. The people responded and left for their homes. "Ah Bradford, Bradford," one man in the crowd said, "you saved him but he will help to burn you one day. If it were not for you, I would have run him through with my sword."

Three days later, constables arrested Bradford and threw him into a dungeon in the Tower of London. They charged him with inciting the people to sedition at St. Paul's Cross. The charge could not have been more false, but Bradford accepted this trial as God's will. "I trust in God," Bradford wrote a friend from prison. "Neither death nor life, prison nor pleasure, shall be able to separate me from my Lord God and His gospel."

Others imprisoned in the Tower at the same time included Bradford's dear friends, Nicholas Ridley and Hugh Latimer, as well as Archbishop Cranmer. The authorities did not want the reformers to communicate with one another, so they kept them in separate cells. However, friends of the prisoners managed to smuggle letters and papers back and forth between them. These leaders of the English Reformation knew that Queen Mary intended to force the doctrines of the Roman church upon all Englishmen. In particular, anyone who denied the physical presence of Christ's body in the Eucharist would be burned at the stake for heresy. They would soon stand trial for their beliefs, and they wanted to defend the faith thoughtfully and boldly from the Word of God. Bradford sought Ridley's advice on a treatise that he was writing against the sacrifice of the mass. Ridley, in turn, sent drafts of his arguments against Roman doctrines for Bradford's comments.

After several months in the Tower, the reformers experienced an unexpected blessing. Many prisoners captured in a failed uprising against the queen swelled the number of inmates in the Tower. To make room, guards threw Latimer, Cranmer, Ridley and Bradford into the same cell. "God be thanked," Latimer said, "it was to our great joy and comfort."

The four men prayed and studied the Scriptures together. In the meantime, the queen got Parliament to pass decrees forcing the people to attend mass under penalty of fine or imprisonment. The queen sent representatives to the pope to seek his forgiveness for England's separation from the Church of Rome.

In March 1554, the queen ordered Latimer, Cranmer and Ridley to stand trial at Oxford University. As guards led them away, they said their final farewells to Bradford. A few days later, Bradford was transferred to the King's Bench prison in another part of London where he awaited his trial. The keeper of the prison, a supporter of the Reformation, granted Bradford the freedom to receive visitors and to preach twice a day. So many came to hear him proclaim the Word of God that his cell filled to overflowing. He often administered the Lord's Supper to those who crowded his chamber for worship. From jail, Bradford wrote his *Exhortation to the Brethren in England* which called on all friends of the Reformation to remain true to the Scriptures. "Pray for all your brethren who are in prison and exile and so absent from you in body but yet present with you in spirit," he wrote. "Heartily pray that God will trust us again with His Holy Word and Gospel."

One reformer said of Bradford, "Such an instrument was he in God's church that those who knew him esteemed him as a precious jewel and God's true messenger." Others called him the "Hearty Gospeller."

In January 1555, after a year and a half of imprisonment, the queen's council ordered Bradford to stand trial before them. "You have been justly imprisoned for your seditious behavior at St. Paul's Cross," Stephen Gardiner, the Lord Chancellor, said, "for your false and arrogant preaching without authority. But now," he added, "the time of mercy is come."

Gardiner told Bradford that the queen would pardon him if he renounced the teachings of the Reformation. "My lords," John Bradford said, "I confess that I have been long imprisoned unjustly, for I did nothing seditiously, falsely or arrogantly, but rather sought truth, peace and all godly quietness."

"I know you have a glorious tongue," Gardiner said mocking-ly, "but all you speak is lies. What do you say now? Will you re-turn again and do as we have done? If you do, you shall receive the queen's mercy and pardon."

"My lord," Bradford answered, "my conscience does not accuse me that I spoke anything for which I should need to receive the queen's mercy or pardon. For everything I spoke was agreeable to God's laws and the laws of the realm."

"Know for truth," Gardiner retorted, "that the queen will rid her realm of men like you. As you have deceived the people with false and devilish doctrine, so shall you receive."

"I have not deceived the people," Bradford responded, "nor taught any other doctrine than, by God's grace, I am ready to con-firm with my life."

"You do nothing but lie," Gardiner said.

"I wish God, the author of truth and abhorrer of lies," Bradford said, "would pull my tongue out of my head before you all, if I have lied to you."

"Heretic!" shouted several members of the court. When they condemned Bradford to death, he fell to his knees and thanked God for counting him worthy to suffer for the sake of Christ. Bailiffs took him back to prison to await burning at the stake.

The court decreed that twenty-year-old John Leaf, an apprentice candle maker, would die with Bradford. Leaf had been arrested for boldly proclaiming his Protestant beliefs. Guards chained Bradford

and Leaf to the stake in Smithfield where a large crowd had gathered to witness the execution. "O England, England, repent of your
sins," Bradford called out. Then he turned to Leaf and said, "Be of
good comfort, brother, for we shall have a merry supper with the
Lord this night."

COMPREHENSION QUESTIONS

for Part Four

1. What strategy did Thomas Bilney use to share Christ with Hugh Latimer?

2. Why was Thomas Bilney burned at the stake?

3. When William Tyndale told a priest, "If God spares my life, in a few years, a ploughboy shall know more of the Scriptures than you do," what did he mean?

4. What hardships did Tyndale face?

5. Why did John Frith return to England in spite of the many dangers, and why did he not flee for his life when given the chance?

6. What did Hugh Latimer make the focal point of his preaching?

7. Why was Hugh Latimer imprisoned in the Tower of London twice?

8. What famous line of encouragement did Latimer say to Ridley at the stake?

9. What were Thomas Cranmer's greatest accomplishments as archbishop of Canterbury?

10. How did Cranmer surprise his persecutors in the church service just before his execution?

11. Explain how Henry VIII could be considered both a supporter of the Reformation and an enemy of it?

12. How did John Bradford comfort his fellow martyr at the stake?

PART FIVE

THE REFORMATION
IN SCOTLAND

Even before news of Martin Luther swept across the North Sea to Scotland, pockets of the Evangelical faith survived in the cottages of the Lollards. They cherished the remnants of their Wyclif Bible and refused to follow the religion of works proclaimed by the Church of Rome. In the 1520s, Patrick Hamilton, a Scottish nobleman, came to a living faith in Christ and began to preach. In 1528, Scottish authorities burned him at the stake for preaching justification by faith in Christ. His clear gospel message and cruel death turned many Scots against the officials of the Roman church. Small groups of people began to meet secretly in homes to pray and study the Scriptures.

In 1546, when the preacher George Wishart was executed under the orders of Cardinal Beaton, the highest church official in the land, Protestant noblemen murdered Beaton and seized his castle in St. Andrews. With the help of French troops, the Scottish crown crushed them, but a growing number of nobles and commoners took up the cause of the Reformation. At that time, Scotland was an independent kingdom separate from England. In 1559, John Knox, the exiled Evangelical preacher, returned to Scotland. Huge crowds came out to hear him as he preached across the length and breadth of the kingdom. In 1560, the Protestants took control of Parliament and severed the Scottish church's ties with Rome. They approved an Evangelical confession of faith, instituted Reformed worship and presbyterian church government in all the churches and established Christian schools throughout the land. The Reformation transformed Scotland as the Spirit of God redeemed hearts and minds.

CHAPTER 27:
PATRICK HAMILTON

Herald of the Scottish Reformation

(1504-1528)

I n the winter of 1528, winds howled off the North Sea through
the grounds of St. Andrews Castle, home of Archbishop James
Beaton. Wrapped in a scarlet fur-lined robe, he paced in front
of the fireplace in the great hall, wondering how to get rid of Patrick Hamilton. Patrick Hamilton, the twenty-four-year-old son of
a wealthy family with close ties to the king of Scotland, had started
preaching. After studying the Greek New Testament as a university
student, Hamilton came to a living faith in Christ and embraced
the ideas of the Reformation. Later, he went to Germany and studied the Scriptures and the writings of Martin Luther and Philip
Melanchthon. Although Hamilton knew that great dangers awaited

him if he returned to Scotland to preach the good news of Christ, he felt compelled to do it out of love for his countrymen.

Back in Scotland, Hamilton proclaimed that sinners could find peace with God only by believing in Christ. "He that lacks faith cannot please God," Hamilton said. His preaching was straightforward, explaining the Scriptures in clear terms. He called everyone to come to Jesus Christ. "It is not sufficient to believe that Christ is a Savior and Redeemer," Hamilton said, "but that he is *your* Savior and *your* Redeemer."

The Church of Rome taught that people found salvation by a combination of belief in God, faithfulness to the rules of the church and good works. "Whoever believes or thinks to be saved by his own works," Patrick Hamilton said, "denies that Christ is his Savior, that Christ died for him. For how is He your Savior if you can save yourself by your own works?"

He made it clear that many works emphasized by the church——pilgrimages, penance, prayers to saints, indulgences and the like——could not be found in the Scriptures. In the corrupt church in Scotland, power-hungry and wealth-grabbing noblemen paid bribes to become bishops or abbots. The church controlled vast tracts of land and collected rents from townspeople and peasants alike. Bishops did not preach or teach and rarely visited the churches that they oversaw. Many ignorant, lazy and immoral priests undermined the church's moral authority.

James Beaton won his seat as archbishop of St. Andrews through a fierce power struggle. Now that Beaton had reached the pinnacle of the Scottish church, he wielded great power and influence in the land, and he used the wealth of the church to live a life of luxury. He didn't want Patrick Hamilton or anyone else changing the church.

Archbishop Beaton feared the Reformation would sweep through Scotland as it had in Germany. Scottish church leaders banned Luther's writings and burned them in the universities. They got the Scottish Parliament to pass a law in 1525 condemning the ideas of the reformers, making it a crime punishable by death to speak or write about them or own their books. In 1526, when Tyndale's New Testament in English began to filter into the country through Scottish ports, they banned it as well. But Reformation ideas kept spreading.

And now Patrick Hamilton, an articulate nobleman with royal blood in his veins and the backing of a powerful family, openly preached Evangelical doctrines. Beaton was determined to stop him. But how could he get his hands on him? Hamilton preached in the homes and churches of the areas controlled by his clan. If Beaton sent men to arrest him, they would meet resistance. So the archbishop resorted to deception. He sent Hamilton a letter inviting him to St. Andrews. "Please come," he wrote, "and we will discuss the state of the church in Scotland and the steps that might be taken to reform her."

Although not deceived by the archbishop's invitation, Patrick Hamilton wanted to witness for Christ in St. Andrews——the center of the Scottish church and home to Scotland's most important university. He told his family before traveling to St. Andrews, "I do not think I have long to live."

Hamilton arrived in St. Andrews in January 1528. Beaton wanted Hamilton to publicly proclaim his views so there would be no question of his heresy. Therefore, he did not arrest Hamilton immediately, but granted him permission to freely teach his beliefs at St. Andrews University and in the churches of the city.

For nearly a month, Hamilton taught the central truths of the Scriptures and openly debated churchmen in the university. The college students had never heard teaching like that before. Hamilton defended his ideas exclusively from the Bible and did not appeal to the writings of church scholars as their professors did. Many people came to him privately. He counseled them to look to Christ to save them from their sins and lead them to a holy life. "We have a good and gentle Lord," he said. "Let us follow His footsteps."

One of the leading monks of St. Andrews, Alexander Alane, visited Hamilton, convinced he could win him back to the faith of the Roman church. However, he met his match in Patrick Hamilton. Not only did Hamilton answer all of his objections from the Word of God, he did so with great kindness and courtesy. Alane returned to his monastery marveling at the wisdom of Hamilton and doubting some of the teachings of the Church of Rome. He conferred with Hamilton several times, and soon Alane put all his trust in Christ's sacrifice for sin.

As Archbishop Beaton built his case against him, Hamilton's friends urged him to flee before he could be arrested by the archbishop. "I came here," Hamilton said, "to strengthen the faith of believers by my death as a martyr to the truth; if I turn back now, I would lay a stumbling block in their path, and might cause some of them to fall."

Not long after, armed guards seized Hamilton at night and threw him in the dungeon of the archbishop's castle. Early the next morning, February 29, 1528, a guard of horsemen led Patrick Hamilton from the castle to St. Andrews Cathedral. A crowd of churchmen and townspeople filled the church. The archbishop led a long train of bishops, abbots and professors in flowing robes into the cathedral and took their seats at the front of the high altar to preside over the heresy trial.

Friar Campbell read the articles of heresy, including that Hamilton had taught that no man is without sin and that a man is not justified by works, but by faith alone. Hamilton happily acknowledged his beliefs and clearly supported them from the Bible. When Campbell found himself silenced by Hamilton's arguments, he turned dumbfounded to the archbishop for direction. "Don't reason with him," Beaton told him, "just bring the accusations!"

Campbell faced Hamilton again and said, "Heretic, you said it's lawful for all men to read the Word of God, especially the New Testament."

"It is lawful for all men to read and understand the Word of God," Hamilton said. "In particular in the New Testament, they can be made to see their sin and repent and come to the mercy of God by faith in Jesus Christ."

"Heretic," continued Friar Campbell, "you say it's not lawful to worship images. Don't you know that images remind the common people of the holy saints that worked for their salvation?"

"Brother," said Hamilton, "it ought to be preaching of the true Word of God that should remind the people of their salvation bought by the blood of Christ."

"Heretic, you say it is worthless to pray to the saints and the Virgin Mary and Peter and Paul as mediators to God for us."

"I say with Paul," Hamilton answered, "there is no mediator between God and men, but Christ Jesus."

"Heretic," Campbell said, "you say that all our efforts to help the souls of our departed from the pains of purgatory are in vain."

"Brother," Hamilton said, "I have never read in the Scripture of such a place as purgatory. The only thing that may purge the souls of men is the blood of Jesus Christ."

The church tribunal condemned Hamilton as a heretic and made arrangements to execute him the same day. At noon, several thousand armed men marched him from the castle to a stake driven into the ground in front of St. Salvador College. When Hamilton reached the place of execution, he gave his New Testament and his coat to a friend, saying, "These will not profit me in the fire; but they will profit you. My death will be an entrance to eternal life, which no one shall possess that denies Christ Jesus before this wicked generation."

Officials of the archbishop stood by the stake. One of them called out, "You may save your life if you recant your errors that you professed this morning in the cathedral."

"I am content that my body burn in this fire for my faith in Christ, than my soul should burn in the fire of hell for denying it," Hamilton said. "I trust in the mercy of God."

A light rain fell as the executioners tied Hamilton to the stake by wrapping an iron chain around his waist and surrounded him with straw, coal and wood. When guards ignited the pile, the flames leapt up for a moment and then smoldered. Instead of a sudden death, Hamilton suffered through six excruciating hours. Despite the pain, Hamilton spoke to the crowd, imploring them to look to Christ. The people who watched the terrible scene marveled that Hamilton never grew impatient or angry.

Hamilton's witness did not end at the stake. People throughout the land asked, "Why was Master Patrick Hamilton burned?" Hamilton's writings——which explained simply the Christian faith from the Scriptures——were printed secretly and widely distributed in Scotland. Alexander Alane, the monk whom Hamilton had led to the Lord, taught the monks at the Priory of St. Andrews what Hamilton had taught him.

Some of the leading professors at St. Andrews University and many of the students, convinced by Hamilton's arguments and by his manly death, turned to Christ with a believing heart. A priest named Henry Forrest was burned at the stake for reading the

English New Testament and for having said, "Patrick Hamilton was no heretic."

As the number of Scots who followed the reformer grew, one gentleman advised Archbishop Beaton to stop burning heretics in public. "My Lord," he said, "the smoke of Master Patrick Hamilton has infected as many as it blew upon."

John Knox, the great reformer who lived to see Hamilton's beliefs embraced by the Church of Scotland, called Patrick Hamilton "The Herald of the Scottish Reformation."

CHAPTER 28:
GEORGE WISHART

A Man of Such Graces
(c.1513–1546)

n the summer of 1545 in Dundee, Scotland, a large crowd listened to a preacher named George Wishart. For several weeks, the tall young man with a black beard had proclaimed the saving grace of Christ. On this day, hundreds packed the church to hear Wishart explain how Christ's sinless life and death won eternal life for all who believe. "Everyone who comes to Christ by faith will never be turned away," he told them.

Suddenly, a city magistrate bounded down the center aisle, waving a writ in his hand. "In the queen's name you are forbidden to preach in Dundee. Be gone and trouble us no more!" As the magistrate read the order against him, Wishart kept silent. Then he turned to the man and said, "God is my witness that I preached at hazard of my life in order to bring peace and not trouble. But I am sure that to reject the Word of God and to drive away His messengers is not the way to save you from trouble."

"Protest the order and keep teaching us the Word of God," many in Dundee told him. But Wishart obeyed the order and left the city at once. He went to western Scotland and began to preach in Ayr.

Six years earlier, he had been a schoolmaster. When the leaders of the Scottish church discovered that Wishart taught his students to read the Greek New Testament, they charged him with heresy. Wishart, knowing that if convicted, he would be killed, fled the country. He traveled to Germany, Switzerland and England to learn the Scriptures from the Evangelical reformers. In England, he taught for a time at Cambridge University where he became well known for his clear explanation of the Scriptures and his kindness to others— giving food and clothing each week to the poor. But Wishart longed to return to Scotland to preach to his countrymen forgiveness and new life in Jesus Christ which so gladdened his own heart.

So in 1544, Wishart went back to Scotland. Great crowds turned out to hear his clear and earnest preaching. He told them that salvation was found in Christ alone, by the grace of God alone, by faith alone. He gave them great hope in God's power to save. But Cardinal David Beaton, who became the head of the church in Scotland when his uncle Archbishop James Beaton died, hated the message that Wishart proclaimed. The church in Scotland, controlled by the pope in Rome, forbade the people to study the Bible for themselves. It taught that a person reached heaven by a combination of faith in God, good works, obedience to the church and a time of suffering in purgatory after death.

When George Wishart arrived in Ayr, the people flocked to hear him preach about a loving Savior. Many put their hope and trust in Jesus Christ, rejoicing in the forgiveness of their sins. As growing crowds attended his preaching, Cardinal Beaton and the bishops plotted to silence him. One day when Wishart was scheduled to preach, the archbishop of Glasgow arrived at the church early, took over the pulpit and posted guards at the church door to keep Wishart out. Some leading men of the town wanted to remove the archbishop by force. "No," Wishart said, "let the archbishop give his sermon here. I will go to the market cross and preach there."

Leaving an empty church to the fuming archbishop, the people filled the town square around the market cross, and Wishart preached. On the following Lord's Day, Wishart was invited to preach in a church in a nearby town. But during the night the sheriff of Ayr placed a guard of armed men around the church. The townsfolk wanted to burst through the guard, but Wishart shook his head and said, "It is the word of peace which I preach to you and the blood of no man shall be shed for it this day. Christ is as mighty in the fields as in the church. Christ preached more often in the desert and at the seaside, than in the temple."

Leading the crowd to a nearby meadow, Wishart climbed atop a stone fence and preached to them for three hours. Several people turned to Christ, including one of the most wicked noblemen in the land who prayed with tears running down his cheeks.

Then Wishart got word that a deadly plague had broken out in Dundee, sweeping scores to their deaths every day. Wishart decided to return to Dundee. The people of Ayr advised him to remain with them saying, "It is too dangerous to return to Dundee, the cardinal will kill you."

"They are now in trouble, and they need comfort," Wishart said. In Dundee, he preached Christ and the joys of heaven to the sick and terrified people. "His message," one man said, "so raised up the hearts of all that heard it that they judged that those who died were happier than those who lived."

While most priests and town leaders had fled the city, Wishart went house to house, caring for the sick and grieving. He organized the distribution of food, winning the love and respect of the citizens. But Cardinal Beaton kept scheming to destroy him. Beaton bribed a priest to assassinate Wishart. The priest came to a service where Wishart preached and stood at the foot of the pulpit steps, hiding a dagger under his cloak. As Wishart came down the steps, he noticed the priest fidgeting nervously with a strange look on his face. Wishart seized the priest hands, snatched his weapon and asked, "What do you intend to do?"

The man fell at his feet and confessed that the cardinal had paid him to kill Wishart. Enraged congregants tried to drag him away saying, "Give the traitor to us!" Wishart stopped them. Raising the man up and embracing him, he said, "Whoever harms him harms me. He did not hurt me. But he gave us all a great warning. In the future, we must watch carefully."

For a few days Wishart went into hiding, but he felt that he was hiding the light of Christ. "I have labored to bring people out of darkness, but now I lurk as a man ashamed to show himself before men."

He decided to preach at Haddington, the hometown of John Knox, a teacher who left his work to become a bodyguard for Wishart. As Wishart left the church, he told Knox to go home. "Return to your students and may God bless you," he said. That night as Wishart slept at the home of a friend, a troop of armed men captured him, hauled him to Beaton's castle in St. Andrews and cast him into the dungeon. Four weeks later, he stood trial before a panel of bishops.

A priest named John Lauder read the charges, accusing Wishart of crimes and heresies. He spit in Wishart's face and cried, "You traitor, you thief, what answer do you give to these charges which we have duly approved by sufficient witnesses against you?"

"I never taught any doctrines contrary to the Ten Commandments or the Apostles' Creed or the Lord's Prayer," Wishart answered. "Since I returned to Scotland, I taught the people in their own language and primarily preached from Paul's letter to the Romans. I implore you to hear me out. I will preach the Word of God to you as I did in Dundee so God may be glorified and that you may judge my teaching fairly."

As Cardinal Beaton and the bishops counseled together, one said, "If we let him preach, he is so crafty and knows the Holy Scripture so well, that he will persuade the people to his opinion and turn them against us."

"You may not preach," they told him. "You may only answer yes or no to each charge presented."

"I desire the Word of God to be my judge," Wishart said.

"False heretic," Lauder continued, "you have denied the power of the pope and said that every layman is a priest."

"On the authority of God's Word," Wishart said, "I taught that believers are 'a holy priesthood,' and those who are ignorant of the Scriptures——whatever their rank or degree——cannot instruct others."

"You have taught, you false heretic, that we should not pray to saints but to God only."

"St. Paul writes that there is only 'one mediator between God and men, the man Christ Jesus,'" Wishart replied. "We are never taught in Scripture to pray to saints."

"False heretic," Lauder said, "you teach that there is no purgatory."

Wishart answered, "If you have any testimony of the Scriptures by which you may prove that purgatory exists, show it to all of us here."

At the end of the proceedings, the bishops declared him guilty and turned him over to the civil authorities to be burned to death.

The next day, March 1, 1546, guards bound him with an iron chain to a large post just outside the castle wall within view of the cardinal's rooms. Cardinal Beaton invited the bishops to watch the execution from the windows of his castle chambers. His servants laid out pillows so the churchmen could watch the burning in comfort.

"I preached to you," Wishart told the crowd of onlookers, "not cunningly devised fables but the true gospel of Christ. I suffer this fire for Christ's sake, not sorrowfully but with a glad heart and mind. This great fire I fear not; and so I pray you to do, if any persecution should come to you for the Word's sake, not to fear them that slay the body, but rather Him who has power to slay the soul."

When the executioner made everything ready for the fire, Wishart said, "I am assured that my soul will this night be with my Savior in heaven." Then he prayed, "I beseech you heavenly Father, forgive them who out of ignorance have condemned me to death this day. I forgive them with all my heart."

The executioner said to him, "I pray your forgiveness, for I am not guilty of your death." Wishart kissed his cheek and said, "I forgive you——do your duty."

Although Cardinal Beaton and the bishops exalted in his execution, the people saw Wishart as a martyr, not a heretic. They began to view church leaders as enemies of the Scriptures.

Not long after, John Knox took up the preaching work of his martyred friend. Years later, when the Reformation was firmly established in the land, Knox wrote of Wishart, "Never before in Scotland was there a man of such graces."

REFORMATION BASICS 7

Key Statements of Faith of the Reformation

As the Reformation progressed, it became important to state its essential beliefs in a clear and concise form. Three of the most important of these statements of faith were the Augsburg Confession, the Heidelberg Catechism and the Thirty-nine Articles.

In 1530, when Emperor Charles V was pressuring German princes to conform to the teaching of the Church of Rome, the Protestant princes called for a statement of the Evangelical faith. It fell to Philip Melanchthon to be its primary author with help from Luther and others. The statement, which became known as the Augsburg Confession, explained from the Bible what Christians are to believe concerning many important biblical themes including God, man, sin, salvation, sacraments and good works. It is the most important of the German Lutheran statements of faith.

The Thirty-nine Articles of the Church of England developed out of the Forty-two Articles, a statement of faith written by Archbishop Thomas Cranmer during the rule of Edward VI. Later, after Elizabeth I began her reign, they were revised and shortened. Since Elizabeth hoped to unite Evangelicals and Roman Catholics in the Protestant Church of England, most of the articles are written broadly to be accepted by as many people as possible. They established the Scripture as the sole authority for doctrine. The Articles are the foundational confession of faith for Anglican churches throughout the world.

In 1562, Frederick, a German prince whose capital was Heidelberg, commissioned Casper Olevianus and Zacharias Ursinus to write a statement of faith that would explain to his subjects Reformed theology——the teachings of the Scriptures by the Swiss and French reformers, especially John Calvin. The Heidelberg Catechism, written in the first person, exudes a joyful personal trust in Jesus Christ, covering God's grace in the heart of a believer from the conviction of sin to trusting Christ to living a thankful, obedient life. It remains a cornerstone description of the Reformed faith to this day.

CHAPTER 29:
WALTER MILL

The Last Protestant Martyr of Scotland
(c. 1476–1559)

———————

In 1559, agents of the archbishop of St. Andrews finally captured their prey—Walter Mill, a man they considered to be one of the most dangerous scoundrels in Scotland. Mill did not look like an enemy of law and order. The eighty-two-year-old Mill, stooped and wrinkled with age, carried no weapon but the Bible. His crime: he taught the people that salvation came only by faith in Jesus Christ and that forgiveness was a gift of God's free grace, not a result of priestly pardons or pilgrimages or good works. He believed that priests should have the right to marry and that Christ instituted just two sacraments——baptism and the Lord's Supper——not the seven sacraments of the Roman church.

Mill had been a Scottish priest for years when the reformer Patrick Hamilton was burned to death in St. Andrews. He, like many of his countrymen, wondered why Hamilton had to die. Mill read Hamilton's writings, and then he started studying the Scriptures for himself. Soon, Mill proclaimed to his parishioners that Jesus paid the price and took the full punishment for the sins of all who believe in Him. In 1538, when the archbishop accused him of heresy and summoned him to appear before a tribunal, Mill fled Scotland to escape the certain flames of the stake. He studied under the reformers of Germany. Mill renounced the Roman priesthood and got married.

After many years in Germany, he felt God's call to return to Scotland and preach the redeeming love of Jesus for sinners. In 1556, he slipped back into Scotland and started teaching and preaching in private homes, never staying too long in one place to avoid the archbishop's agents. But in 1559, they captured him in a little town in Fife and hauled him twenty miles to the archbishop's castle in St. Andrews. The archbishop wanted to get Mill to forsake his Protestant faith in order to save his life, hoping a public recantation would hurt the Evangelical cause and strengthen the Church of Rome.

Inquisitors threatened Mill with ghastly tortures if he refused to recant, but Mill held fast to his faith. Then they tried flattery. "Sir Walter, you are an ordained priest of the church," one interrogator told him. "If you would simply sign this recantation, you would be welcomed back into the fold. You would receive room and board at Dunfermline Abbey, where you could spend your remaining days in prayer and study."

Mill rejected the offer out of hand.

With no hope of a recantation, the archbishop summoned a panel of bishops, abbots and theologians from across Scotland to judge the case at St. Andrews Cathedral. On April 20, 1559, spectators jammed the church to witness the trial of the accused heretic. They were shocked to see a feeble old man standing in the dock. When Mill was commanded to go up into the pulpit to answer the charges, he needed help to mount the stairs. At the top, Mill dropped to his knees and prayed silently. After a few minutes, the chief questioner, a priest named Oliphant, grew impatient and said, "Sir Walter Mill, arise and give answers to the articles against you."

Mill slowly lifted himself up. He smiled and said in a clear voice, "We ought to obey God rather than men. You call me Sir Walter——do not call me that any longer. I have been one of the pope's knights for too long."

"What do you think about priests' marriage?" Oliphant asked.

"I believe it is a blessed union, for Christ Himself approved it and made it free to all men," Mill answered.

"You say there are not seven sacraments," Oliphant added.

"Give me the Lord's Supper and baptism, and you take the rest," Mill replied.

"You deny the sacrament of the altar to be the very body and blood of Christ," Oliphant charged.

"The mass is wrong," Mill said, "because Christ was offered once on the cross for man's trespass and will never be offered again. He ended all sacrifice on the cross."

"You preach against pilgrimage," Oliphant said.

"I say it is not commanded in the Scripture," he answered.

"You preach secretly and privately in houses and openly in the fields."

"Yes, indeed!" Mill replied. "And also on the sea, sailing in a ship."

"Will you recant your errors?" Oliphant asked. "If you do not, we will pronounce sentence against you."

"I stand accused for my life," Mill said. "I know I must die once. Therefore, I say to you what Christ said to Judas, 'What you do, do quickly.' I will not recant the truth."

When the questioning ended, the judges condemned him to death as an obstinate heretic. Since the church lacked the legal right to put anyone to death, they delivered Mill over to the secular authorities to execute him by burning at the stake. However, the government leaders and nearly all the citizens of St. Andrews were in sympathy with Mill, believing it would be a crime to put the learned old man to death. When the archbishop could not find a government official willing to carry out Mill's execution, he bribed a man on his own staff to act as a temporary judge. Even then, the archbishop's men could not find a soul in the city willing to sell them the rope with which to bind Mill to the stake or the wood with which to burn him. They had to tear apart the archbishop's pavilion to get the necessary supplies for the execution.

As guards tied Mill to the stake, he asked if he could address the spectators. "No," his persecutors replied. But the people demanded that Mill be heard. Fearing the crowd's wrath, they let him speak. With his back bound to the stake, he called out, "The cause for which I suffer this day is not for any crime——although I admit that I am a miserable sinner——but only for the defense of the truth that is in Jesus Christ. I praise God who has called me by His mercy to seal the truth with my life. As God has given me my life, so I willingly and joyfully offer it up to His glory. Therefore, if you are to escape eternal death, do not be seduced any longer by the lies of priests, friars, abbots, bishops and the rest of the sect of Antichrist, but depend solely on Jesus Christ and His mercy so that you may be delivered from condemnation."

As the flames rose, he said, "I trust I shall be the last one in Scotland to suffer death for the Christian faith."

When word of Mill's cruel death spread across the kingdom, a wave of indignation against church leaders swept over the Scots. Wanting to preserve the memory of Walter Mill's faithful testimony, the people of St. Andrews built a great heap of stones on the spot where he was burned. The archbishop had the stones removed and threatened punishment upon anyone who dared to replace the stones. But it was all in vain, for the stone memorial would reappear as quickly as it was pulled down.

"Out of Mill's ashes," wrote John Foxe, "sprang thousands of his faith in Scotland." Less than two years after the death of Walter Mill, the Scottish Reformation threw out the archbishop of St. Andrews and his ilk. And the doctrines for which Mill died became the creed of the Church of Scotland. He was the last Protestant martyr in Scotland during the Reformation era.

CHAPTER 30:
JOHN KNOX

He Never Feared the Face of Man
(c. 1514–1572)

n January 1546, John Knox anxiously stood guard in his hometown church in Haddington, Scotland, while his friend George
Wishart preached. Twice in the last month, Cardinal Beaton,
the most powerful churchman in Scotland, had sent assassins to kill
Wishart. Knox, a tutor to the sons of a Scottish laird, served as a
bodyguard armed with a two-handed sword to protect the Evangelical preacher. An hour before the sermon, Wishart had sent for him.
With dark circles under his eyes and his head drooped, Wishart
sighed, "Master John, I am weary of this world because the people
are growing weary of God."

After the sermon, when the congregation departed, Knox told
Wishart that he would accompany him on the road to the place

where he planned to spend the night. "No," Wishart said, taking the sword from Knox's hands, "return to your students, and may God bless you. One is sufficient for a sacrifice."

Reluctantly, Knox departed, full of foreboding for his friend. That night, armed guards arrested Wishart and threw him into the dungeon of the cardinal's castle in St. Andrews. A few weeks later, George Wishart was burned at the stake outside the cardinal's window so that he and other high church officials could watch him suffer.

Wishart's cruel execution turned many Scots against Cardinal Beaton and the Church of Rome, and ignited the ire of some Scottish nobles for revenge. Meanwhile, Beaton plotted to crush the leading noblemen who favored the Protestant faith, but they struck him first. A band of nobles, seeking to avenge the death of Wishart, stormed Beaton's castle and killed him. They hung his body from the window where he had watched Wishart burn.

Church officials and the Scottish crown reacted swiftly to the assassination. They ordered the arrest of Evangelical leaders, including John Knox. To avoid capture, Knox hid himself and moved from place to place. Then the laird for whom he had worked prevailed on Knox to bring his sons to the safety of St. Andrews Castle which was still held by the Protestant nobles. When Knox and his pupils arrived at the castle, he taught them their subjects and lectured to them from the Scriptures. Knox so impressed the men in the castle that they urged him to preach publicly. But Knox, having a high view of God's calling to the ministry, refused, saying, "I will not run where God has not called me."

Then one Sunday, after the chief preacher in the castle finished his sermon on the calling of ministers, he turned to Knox and said, "Brother, I and all here charge you in the name of God and His

Son Jesus Christ not to refuse the holy vocation of building up your brothers and sisters in Christ through the public office of preaching."

"Is this your charge to me?" Knox asked. "It is," the people answered.

Knox burst into tears and ran from the church. A few days later, he overcame his reticence and began to preach. His hearers marveled at his forceful preaching and his deep knowledge of the Scriptures. In the churches of St. Andrews, the people could hear the priests of the Church of Rome or Knox and the other Evangelical preachers. The priests called the Evangelicals "heretics" and ordered the people not to listen to them. Knox challenged the priests and friars that he could prove from the Bible the truth of Protestant teaching and the errors of the Roman church. Public debates were held in a parish church of the town and in the university. The townspeople packed the church to hear Knox debate the friars and the deans of the university. Knox argued from the Word of God, quoting passages from the gospels and the epistles to prove his points. The proponents of the Roman church quoted medieval theologians and kept saying, "The Roman church is the infallible authority and its teachings must be obeyed. No further discussion is necessary."

Knox told them that no one should follow the church's teachings if they were not supported by Scripture. "If we follow your teaching," one friar said, "you will leave us no church."

"If you remain in your church," Knox replied, "I cannot stop you, but as for me, I will be in no other church but that which has Jesus Christ for her pastor, hears His voice, and will not listen to the voice of a stranger."

Many people in St. Andrews threw off the shackles of striving to earn God's favor through their own good works or through the merits of the saints and trusted Christ alone to make them right with God. The rulers of Scotland, fearful of losing power to the

Protestants, petitioned France for help. Ships of the French navy attacked St. Andrews Castle and captured Knox and scores of other Evangelicals and condemned them to the slave galleys. In prison rags and leg irons, Knox found himself on the French galley, *Nostre Dame*. Chained night and day to the rowing bench, the slaves felt the crack of slave drivers' whips across their backs and suffered exposure to sun, wind, and rain. They barely survived on scanty rations of biscuits and water. Disease swept through the crowded galleys, and most men died within a year or two. "The torment I suffered in the galleys," Knox said later, "brought forth sobs of my heart." Though battered and bruised, his faith in God remained unshaken.

At one time, the *Nostre Dame* traveled across to Scotland and a fellow Scottish prisoner said to Knox, "Look ashore, can you tell where we are?" Knox, lifting himself from the rough wooden bench, craning his neck and peering over the deck, caught a glimpse of the tower of St. Andrews Cathedral. "Yes, I know it well," Knox said, "for I see the steeple of that place where God first opened my mouth in public to His glory, and I know, no matter how weak I am now, that I shall not die until I shall glorify His godly name there again."

After nearly two years in chains, France released Knox due to the intervention of English Protestants. Since he would be put to death if he returned to Scotland, Knox went to England to help advance the Reformation there. His dynamic preaching won the admiration of King Edward VI who invited Knox to preach regularly before the royal court. Knox, who only a few months before rowed in a slave galley, now proclaimed God's Word to kings and princes.

When King Edward died suddenly, Mary Tudor took the throne, vowing to return England to the Church of Rome. "Bloody Mary" sentenced hundreds of Protestants to death. Knox fled to Switzerland, befriending John Calvin in Geneva. The Genevan church welcomed Evangelical refugees from all over Europe and generously provided for their needs. Knox pastored a church of English-speaking refugees, and he closely observed the Reformed teaching and presbyterian government of the Genevan church. "It is the most perfect school of Christ on earth since the days of the apostles," he said.

Knox longed to return home and proclaim the good news of forgiveness in Christ to the benighted Scots. "I feel a sob and groan," Knox said, "wanting to preach Christ Jesus openly in my native country, although it should be with the loss of my wretched life." He kept in contact by letter with the Evangelicals of Scotland, urging them to hold fast to Christ. In 1555, he slipped into Scotland for a few months and ministered secretly to those who longed for a reformed church. Knox called them to form congregations and worship in secret until the time was right for a Protestant Reformation in the land.

Then in 1559, after twelve years in exile, Knox returned to Scotland with the support of the growing number of Evangelical nobles. During his absence, church leaders condemned him as a heretic, and the crown declared him an outlaw and offered a reward for his capture——dead or alive. Anyone who listened to Knox did so under pain of death. Yet when John Knox arrived in Scotland, huge crowds rushed out to greet him and hear him preach. He spoke plainly, yet with great passion, inspiring the Scots to worship Christ according to the Scripture. "By God's grace," Knox said, "I declare Jesus Christ, the strength of His death and the power of His resurrection." He kept on the move, preaching throughout the kingdom. And Scots turned to Christ by the thousands——nobles and shepherds, men and women, boys and girls. Many monks and priests, too, trusted Christ to save their souls from the wrath of God and to bring them to heaven.

When Knox planned to preach in St. Andrews, the archbishop warned him that if he did, he would send troops to shoot him. Protestant nobles advised Knox not to go. "We do not have enough supporters in St. Andrews to protect you," they told him. "It might lead to the sacrifice of your life."

"Do not be afraid of the danger that may come to me," Knox told them, "for my life is in the custody of God whose glory I seek. I do not desire the hand or weapon of any man to defend me. I only crave to preach to the people."

The next day, Knox stood in the pulpit of St. Andrews Cathedral to speak to a great crowd. He pointed them to Christ who took the punishment due to sinners on Himself on the cross. Knox also exposed the corruptions and unbiblical practices of the Roman church. For the next three days, he preached in St. Andrews without opposition. Knox praised God for His faithfulness, remembering the day he had seen the tower of St. Andrews Cathedral from the slave ship so many years before. His messages so affected the townspeople and the magistrates of St. Andrews that they declared in favor of the Reformed faith and stripped the images and pictures from the churches of the city.

"The voice of that one man," a Scot said, "is able in one hour to put more life in us than five hundred trumpets continually blustering in our ears."

The rulers of Scotland, with the help of French troops, tried to crush the Protestants, but they fought back. In the summer of 1560, reformed-minded nobles and members of the Scottish Parliament controlled the government and declared Scotland Protestant, although the monarchy remained loyal to the Church of Rome. Parliament asked Knox to lead a committee of ministers to write a confession of faith for the Scottish church. In less than a week,

Knox's committee completed the Scots Confession——a document that clearly proclaimed that salvation is a gift of God's free grace and is found only in Christ. It declared that the Scriptures alone are the supreme authority of the church. Parliament ratified the Scots Confession as the statement of faith for the realm.

Parliament renounced the rule of the pope and bishops of the Church of Rome and directed Knox and some other ministers to organize the Church of Scotland according to the Scriptures. They laid out biblical guidelines for worship and established a presbyterian system of church government. They called for the churches throughout the land to build Christian schools to educate every Scottish child. Knox wanted churches and schools to be financed from the vast lands formally controlled by the Church of Rome, but nobles who had grabbed much of that land for themselves were unwilling to give it up. Knox preached against the greed and corruption of the ruling class. His forthright sermons made him many enemies.

Although shot at and threatened, Knox pressed on, inspiring the people to hold fast to their faith. Several times, Mary, Queen of Scots, summoned Knox to appear before her. Convinced that she held absolute power to rule her subjects, she despised Knox and the Protestants who taught the people to follow God before any other.

"You are teaching the people to believe things that I have not allowed," she told him. "How can this be right since God commands subjects to obey their rulers?"

"Madam," Knox answered, "Your subjects are not bound to follow what you feel is right, but what God's Word declares to be true." The beautiful young queen expected doting submission from her people, and Knox's blunt remarks turned her creamy cheeks to crimson.

"How dare you speak to me like that!" the queen said, fanning her flushed face. "I have put up with you for too long. I shall be revenged."

"I must obey God," Knox said. "His Word commands me to speak plainly and flatter no one on the face of the earth."

As Knox grew older, he suffered greatly from stomach ailments that came from the harsh treatment he had received in the slave galleys. Although so weak that he had to be carried into the pulpit, he continued preaching to the day of his death. At his funeral, a Scottish noble said, "Here lies one who never feared the face of man."

COMPREHENSION QUESTIONS

for Part Five

1. Why did Archbishop Beaton fear Patrick Hamilton?

2. After Patrick Hamilton was burned at the stake, one advisor to Archbishop Beaton warned him not to publicly burn anymore heretics, saying, "The smoke of Master Hamilton has infected as many as it blew upon." What did he mean?

3. What was there about George Wishart that made John Knox say of him: "Never before in Scotland was there a man of such graces?"

4. Describe Walter Mill at his trial and execution.

5. How did John Knox end up as a slave on a French galley ship?

6. Why is John Knox considered the most important leader of the Scottish Reformation?

FOR FURTHER
READING

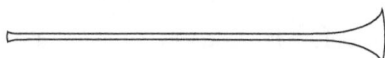

The work of the historian and biographer is highly selective—especially for the writer of biographical sketches. Far more is left out than can be included. To learn much more about the men and women of the Reformation introduced in this book, explore the following sources. Older public domain works are often available free of charge through websites like books. google.com and archive.org.

GENERAL HISTORIES OF THE REFORMATION

The Reformation: A History by Diarmaid MacCulloch, 2003

History of Reformation of the Sixteenth Century by J.H. Merle D'Aubigne, 1843

The Reformation by Owen Chadwick, 1972

The Reformation of the Sixteenth Century by Roland Bainton, 1952

FORERUNNERS OF THE REFORMATION

Girolamo Savonarola by Douglas Bond and Douglas McComas, 2014

Israel of the Alps by Alexis Muston, 1875

John Huss: His Life, Teaching and Death After 500 Years by David Schaff, 1915

John Wycliffe by Ellen Caughey, 2001

The History of Girolamo Savonarola and His Times by Pasquali Villari, 1863

The History of the Waldensians by James Wylie, 1886

The Poor Preachers: The Adventures of the First Lollards by Arthur Bardswell, 2011

GERMANY, SWEDEN AND THE NETHERLANDS

Here I Stand: A Life of Martin Luther by Roland Bainton, 1950

Martin Bucer: Unsung Hero of the Reformation by David Lawrence, 2008

Olavus Petri: Church Reformer of Sweden by Nils Forsander, 1918

The Life of Philip Melanchthon by Karl F. Ledderhose, 2012

William the Silent: William of Nassau, Prince of Orange by C.V. Wedgewood, 1944

FRANCE, SWITZERLAND AND ITALY

For God and His People: Ulrich Zwingli and the Swiss Reformation by M. D'Aubigne and M. Sidwell, 2004

Gaspard de Coligny: Admiral of France by Walter Besant, 1879, reprinted 2016

Lefevre: Pioneer of Ecclesiastical Renewal in France by Philip Edgcumbe Hughes, 1985

John Calvin: Pilgrim and Pastor by Robert Godfrey, 2009

Reformer of Basel: The Life and Thought of Johannes Oecolampadius by Diane Poythress, 2011

Renée of France by Simonetta Carr, 2013

The Pearl of Princesses: Life of Queen Marguerite of Navarre by Hugh Williams, 1916.

William Farel and the Story of the Swiss Reformation by William Blackburn, 1865

ENGLAND

God's Outlaw: The Story of William Tyndale and the English Bible by Brian Edwards, 1987

Hugh Latimer: Foremost Preacher of the English Reformation by Richard Hannula, 2013

John Frith, Scholar and Martyr, a Biography by Brian Raynor, 2000

Masters of the English Reformation by Marcus Loane, 2005

Memoirs of the Life and Martyrdom of John Bradford by John Bradford and William Stevens, 1832

The Acts and Monuments of John Foxe in 8 volumes by John Foxe, 1870.

Thomas Cranmer: A Life by Diarmaid MacCulloch, 1998

SCOTLAND

Seven Men of the Kirk by Beatrice Sawyer, 1959

The History of the Reformation in Scotland by John Knox, 1982

The Life of George Wishart, the Scottish Martyr by Charles Rogers, 1876

John Knox and the Reformation by D.M. Lloyd-Jones & Iain Murray, 2011

WOMEN OF THE REFORMATION

Ladies of the Reformation by James Anderson, 1855.

Radiant: Fifty Remarkable Women in Church History by Richard M. Hannula, 2015

Women and the Reformation by Kirsi Stjerna, 2008

Women of the Reformation in France and England by Roland Bainton, 1975

Women of the Reformation in Germany and Italy by Roland Bainton, 1971

ANSWERS FOR COMPREHENSION QUESTIONS

INTRODUCTION, OVERVIEW, AND PART 1

1. Answers might include: Belief in purgatory, prayers to and veneration of Mary and the saints, the sacrifice of Christ in the mass, the pope as the undisputed head of the church, a process of salvation dependent on good works and the intercession of a priest in the sacraments, seven sacraments, insistence that worship be conducted in Latin and not the language of the people...

2. The invention of the printing press spread new ideas rapidly; the Renaissance revival of classical learning led scholars to question medieval authorities and drew them back to original sources, including studying the New Testament in its original Greek; the power of the pope had weakened while the power of regional and national political leaders had strengthened; the prestige of

the Church of Rome had been weakened through corruption, abuse and immorality.

3. Holy Roman Emperor Charles V, Philip II of Spain, Henry II and Charles IX of France, Mary I of England.

4. Frederick the Wise and John Frederick I of Saxony, Henry VIII and Edward VI and Elizabeth I of England, Philip of Hesse.

5. They looked to the Scriptures alone as the supreme authority for Christians, and they read the Scriptures and conducted worship services in their own language not in Latin, and they did not recognize the pope as the supreme head of the church.

6. Because Wyclif embraced nearly all of the Reformation doctrines 150 years before the Reformation. He rejected transubstantiation and taught that sinners are forgiven only through the grace of God by believing in Christ. He said that indulgences, masses, and pilgrimages do not add to salvation. He translated the Scriptures into the language of the people and challenged the authority of the pope by saying the pope should be followed only in so far as he follows the Scriptures.

7. Influential leaders in England protected him, and the pope who was seeking Wyclif's life died which led to a power struggle in Rome over who would succeed him which allowed Wyclif to carry on for a time.

8. Although the emperor promised Huss protection from harm if he came to Constance, the emperor reneged on his promise. Huss was burned to death because he would not recant his views before the council unless they proved to him from Scripture that his views were in error.

9. Savonarola pointed out Medici's sins of corruption, theft and abuse of power.

10. Church leaders did not like that he was a popular preacher who pointed out errors and abuse in the church, political leaders hated him for exposing their corruptions, and the people did not like his call to repent and live holy lives.

PART 2

1. Saxony was in northern Germany, far away from the pope in Rome and the emperor in Vienna, and Prince Frederick the Wise was an influential leader who enjoyed a measure of independence in the empire.

2. It was nothing more than a scheme for the pope to raise money by preying on people's fears. It also gave people a false hope of God's blessing and forgiveness without pointing them to Christ the true source of their salvation.

3. No, he expected to have a debate among the scholars and churchmen of Wittenberg about indulgences.

4. Because the Diet could not prove from Scripture that his views were contrary to the Bible, so Luther felt bound by his conscience to hold fast to the truths that he had learned from the Word of God.

5. They were Augustinian monks in Antwerp who were converted to faith in Christ alone after reading the writings of Martin Luther. In 1523, when they were burned at the stake in Brussels, they became the first martyrs of the Reformation.

6. Luther was bold, impulsive, headstrong, passionate and combative. Melanchthon was quiet, shy, thoughtful and retiring.

7. He was the author of the *Augsburg Confession*, the most important statement of faith for Lutherans. He also wrote *Commonplaces*, the first Protestant systematic theology, as well as several commentaries on books of the Bible.

8. The grace of God worked in Bucer when he talked with Martin Luther about salvation, and he carefully studied the Scriptures for himself.

9. He worked tirelessly to unite the reformers, to emphasize what they had in common, not what divided them.

10. Because she corresponded with and encouraged many of the leading reformers including Luther, Bucer and Calvin, and gave them hospitality in her home.

11. He preached salvation in Christ alone to the people and exposed errors of the Roman church, he taught in the cathedral seminary, he convinced the king to protect Protestant preachers, he translated the Bible into Swedish and authored a worship book in Swedish.

12. He was one of the principal authors of the Heidelberg Catechism, a warm and beautiful expression of the Reformed faith that was adopted in many lands. It remains a cornerstone statement of the faith to this day.

13. When King Henry II of France revealed a secret plan that he had with King Philip II of Spain to wipe out the Evangelicals of the Netherlands, William remained silent and then raced to the Netherlands to warn the Dutch Evangelicals of the murderous plot.

14. Because he spent his time and treasure leading the Dutch fight against the Spanish who wanted to crush their freedom of worship and their ancient liberties.

PART 3

1. An accurate and eloquent translation of the Bible into French

2. God opened his eyes when he read the New Testament in Greek and carefully studied and memorized the Scriptures.

3. Because he was the first in Switzerland to preach justification by grace through faith in Christ alone, and his preaching led to Zurich being won for the Reformation, from Zurich the Protestant faith spread to many Swiss cantons.

4. He trained and sent out preachers. He encouraged the city fathers of Basel to welcome persecuted French Protestants who fled to Switzerland. From Basel, French Bibles and Evangelical books were printed and smuggled back to France. He encouraged Frenchmen like Farel to preach the good news of Christ.

5. He had to flee his native France for his life. As he preached in the French-speaking parts of Switzerland, he was mocked, beaten, jailed and run out of one town after another.

6. When he was passing through Geneva, William Farel urged him to stay and help him guide the city in the Evangelical faith. When Calvin balked at the idea, Farel told him that God would punish him if he refused to help. So Calvin felt that it was God's will for him to work in Geneva.

7. His book the *Institutes of the Christian Religion* became the most influential book of the Reformation, clearly explaining the central teachings of the Bible. Geneva was a haven for Protestant

refugees from many countries, and they returned to their homelands shaped by Calvin's teaching.

8. When they were being attacked, he became their key military leader in battle who helped the Huguenots win the right to worship in France. After the fighting ended, Coligny served the king in Paris, hoping to get the king to see that the Huguenots were loyal subjects whose rights should be protected.

9. An attack on French Protestants in August, 1572, where thousands were slaughtered by order of the Crown in Paris and around the country.

10. She sent financial support to persecuted Protestant ministers living in exile. She helped reformers like Orchino of Italy to escape persecution, and welcomed reformers who fled to her court for protection.

11. He was calm and steadfast in his faith in Christ. He faced the prospect of death with joy, knowing he would soon be in heaven. He took the opportunity to lead others to Christ with his words at the end.

12. In Italy, no princes embraced the Evangelical faith nor used their power to protect Evangelical preachers. But in Saxony, Luther had the protection of a powerful Protestant prince.

PART 4

1. He went to Latimer's room and asked if Latimer would hear his confession. When Latimer agreed, Bilney told him how he had found faith and new life in Christ when he read the New Testament. His confession was his personal testimony, and God used it to bring Latimer to a living faith in Christ.

2. He was killed for preaching the good news of Christ and exposing the errors of the Church of Rome, and for distributing copies of Tyndale's New Testament in English.

3. Tyndale meant that he hoped to translate the Bible into English so that every man or woman, boy or girl, in the kingdom could read God's Word for themselves.

4. He toiled in exile far from his homeland, translating the Bible into English. Several times he had to flee for his life when his pursuers discovered his whereabouts. He endured a shipwreck and the loss of most of his translation work. He was captured, imprisoned and burned at the stake.

5. Frith felt compelled to return to England and preach the good news of Christ to his countrymen even though it was likely he would be killed for it. After he was arrested, he did not escape when given the opportunity because he wanted to defend Evangelical teaching by using Scripture before the English court. His conscience told him that if he ran away, he would be running from God.

6. Salvation is a gift of God's free grace through Christ's victory on the cross.

7. The first time he was sent there by Henry VIII when Latimer refused to sign a list of beliefs that he found contrary to Scripture that the king and Parliament were forcing on the bishops. The second time he was sent there by Queen Mary who wanted to destroy Protestantism in England and planned to kill the Evangelical leaders of the kingdom.

8. "Be of good cheer, Master Ridley, and play the man. We shall this day, by God's grace, light such a candle in England, as I trust, will never be put out."

9. Cranmer won King Henry VIII's approval to have the Bible
    published in English and placed in every church in the land.
    Under King Edward, Cranmer abolished the Latin mass in En-
    gland and replaced it with a service in English based on the
    Book of Common Prayer which Cranmer wrote. He wrote the
    Forty-two Articles, a biblical statement of faith for the Church
    of England.

10. He publicly renounced his recantation and died proclaiming his
    allegiance to the Word of God and the Evangelical cause.

11. He acted as an enemy to the Reformation when before his first
    divorce, he had written against Luther and openly persecuted
    Protestants in his realm and after he separated the Church of
    England from the Church of Rome he refused to allow Protes-
    tant reformers the opportunity to thoroughly reform the church.
    He acted as a supporter of the Reformation by separating the
    Church of England from the power of the pope and making the
    reformer, Thomas Cranmer, archbishop of Canterbury and per-
    mitting the Scriptures to be published in English and allowing
    his son to be influenced by Protestant regents.

12. He told him that "We shall have a merry supper with the Lord
    this night."

PART 5

1. Because Hamilton was a well-educated nobleman whose fam-
    ily was close to the king and Hamilton was boldly preaching
    Evangelical doctrines, and Beaton feared the Church of Rome
    in Scotland would be overturned if Hamilton continued.

2. He meant that Hamilton's gospel message, his godly charac-
    ter and his bravery at the stake inspired people to follow his
    teaching.

3. Knox probably had in mind, Wishart's faithful gospel preach-
    ing, his kindness, his desire for peace, and his care and sacrifice
    for the poor and sick.

4. The eighty-two-year-old Mill was bold and quick witted at his
    trial, holding fast to his faith in Christ and the cause of Protes-
    tantism. He was unwavering in his testimony for Christ at the
    stake and won the respect of the crowd who witnessed his death.

5. He had been living and preaching at St. Andrews Castle when
    the French navy, in league with the Catholic monarch of Scot-
    land, attacked the castle and took Knox and many others
    prisoner.

6. Because his preaching won thousands to Christ. He encouraged
    reform-minded nobles and members of Parliament to declare
    Scotland a Protestant state. He led the writing of the Scots Con-
    fession, the Evangelical statement of faith for Scotland. He and
    other ministers organized the Church of Scotland as a Presbyte-
    rian system of church government, trained Protestant ministers,
    and promoted the building of Christian schools throughout the
    land.

www.ingramcontent.com/pod-product-compliance
Lightning Source LLC
LaVergne TN
LVHW051727080426
835511LV00018B/2922